17721

D1105793

HOW TO IMPROVE YOUR TENNIS

Style, Strategy, and Analysis

Also by Craig R. Wilson:

The Tennis Player's Profile
The Player Interaction Analysis

HOW TO IMPROVE YOUR TENNIS
Style, Strategy, and Analysis

Craig R. Wilson

SOUTH BRUNSWICK AND NEW YORK: A. S. BARNES AND COMPANY
LONDON: THOMAS YOSELOFF LTD

17721

A. S. Barnes and Co., Inc.
Cranbury, New Jersey 08512

Thomas Yoseloff Ltd
108 New Bond Street
London W1Y OQX, England

Library of Congress Cataloging in Publication Data

Wilson, Craig R
    How to improve your tennis: style, strategy, and analysis.

    1.   Tennis.   I.   Title.
GV995.W73   796.34'22   73-17465
ISBN 0-498-01483-5

PRINTED IN THE UNITED STATES OF AMERICA

For my father, a constant source of inspiration
and
my children, Tonya Helen and Craig Leland, so that they might
always know the Wilson Way

This book is dedicated to those who
OPPOSED and inadvertently clarified
SUPPORTED but did not understand
UNDERSTOOD and supported because of it
QUESTIONED and thereby redirected
SUGGESTED and thus expanded
ACTED INTUITIVELY but did not fear scientific interpretation
ACTED SCIENTIFICALLY but did not falter when proof wore thin

CONTENTS

Self confidence

ACKNOWLEDGMENTS

My sincerest thanks go to:

Jacki Wilson, my wife, for support to a preoccupied husband.

Helen Wilson, my mother, as my most ardent supporter.

Dr. L. Craig Wilson, my father, for his invaluable editorial advice.

Marilyn and Bill Lubel, for their support and creation of the free and unhindered environment from which this work arose.

Al and Peggy Tenhundfeld, and their son Mark, the first apostle of the Wilson Way.

Joy Mitchell, who showed me more than any, the intangible rewards of teaching.

Bob Whelove, for his encouragement and support of the systems-analysis concept.

Fred Rux, for his artistic job in drawing the *Tennis Players Profile* and *Player Interaction Analysis*.

Margaret Varner, Margaret O. DuPont and Ed Garcia for their valuable coaching efforts.

Newton Cox, as the man who sold me on tennis as a profession.

Dr. C. Roy Rylander, for his editorial advice.

Gale Fly, for research references.

Patti Krause and Kathy Moore, for their very efficient typing of the final manuscript.

The photographs of the Wilson method were taken by Pierre Mouyal.

INTRODUCTION

How To Improve Your Tennis is the first conceptual model to encompass the game of tennis in its entirety—style, strategy, and analysis.

The book progresses systematically from the practical aspects of sound stroke development, through a detailed study of percentage decision-making on the court, to the strategy and tactics necessary to compete successfully in tournament-level competition, and concludes with the first theoretical model to objectify both individual career development (the *Tennis Player's Profile*) and competition performance (the *Player Interaction Analysis*).

The literature of tennis is sparse. Folklore treats the game as an art form—which it is, in part. However, it is also a system of precision moves that are subject to scientific study and analysis. By providing a comprehensive model for the latter, and simultaneously offering profuse illustrations of the former, the book invites further development in both the art and the science of tennis.

HOW TO IMPROVE YOUR TENNIS

Style, Strategy, and Analysis

Part I. Technique and Style:
The Aesthetic Quality of the Game

There is a certain aesthetic quality to the game of tennis when it is executed properly. The body flows rhythmically in seemingly effortless motion as the player engages in the mental exchange of attack and defense. The method of stroke execution described in this book seeks to instill an unimposed rhythm to the student, an economical swing that will accomplish as much work for the player as possible with a minimum amount of energy spent, while at the same time allowing him to retain a unique quality of individualism that is valuable and peculiar only to himself. The great players do not look alike as they swing because they have all adapted to their own given abilities and talents. Many of these players resemble one another, however, since there are certain essential characteristics that do remain strikingly the same. It is these elements that the inspired teacher should recognize and seek to instill in his students. The essential elements of such a swing are *balance* and the development of a *fluid motion*. The tennis player is constantly on the move and is, therefore, always presented with the problem not only of positioning himself in correct relation to a moving ball, but of maintaining his balance throughout the shot as well. The fluid swing is a motion that is smooth and rhythmic, simple and without wasted movement, and one that generates its force through the wise use of racket momentum and applied laws of physics.

The aesthetic quality of the game and the development of smooth stroke execution are not attained through off-the-cuff reflection or a casual approach to the learning process. The close observation and scientific study that resulted in the development of this book has revealed that there are two fundamental schools of thought concerning stroke execution in tennis today, and how it should be taught. One method is the *straight backswing*, and the other is the *loop* or semielliptical theory, as advocated by this book. It has been my experience that many people cling to the misconception that the word *loop* is synonymous with *circle*, and it is from this mistaken judgment that proponents of the straight backswing draw their fundamental, but faulty, argument: that being that the player does not have sufficient time to execute such a swing in today's fast and agressive games. Nothing could be further from the truth since, when done properly, it does not constitute a circle. It is made with the racket head, not the arm, and is readily attained as one lowers the racket naturally from the pivot position to the level of the ball. This "C" swing facilitates the development of a rhythmic motion and allows acceleration of the racket head, a fact that contributes to the seemingly effortless stroke execution of such great champions as Ken Rosewall and the graceful Evonne Goolagong. The straight backswing segments the motion by coming to a stop in the back and requires far more effort to complete, since it requires energy to draw the racket back, energy to bring it to a stop, and still more to restart the forward motion. High speed films have shown that segmented motions of this type have required as much as 39% more time to complete, a fact that results primarily from the lack of accelerated motion inherent in the more desirable loop backswing. For the competitive player, where physical condition and the economical use of a given amount of energy often make the ultimate difference between winning and losing, a sound swing without wasted motion becomes invaluable. A semielliptical swing on the ground strokes accomplishes this end better than any. A systematic discussion of the essential characteristics of all of the strokes now follows.

1

THE FOREHAND DRIVE

The forehand drive is usually the first stroke mastered by the beginner, and often remains the dominant stroke for even the best of players. Those players noted for forehand excellence, in the style advanced by this book, include the great Australian champions Frank Sedgeman, Ken Rosewall, and Rod Laver and Americans Jack Kramer, Pancho Gonzalez, and Stan Smith. All have been world-class competitors who developed highly aggressive but very efficient styles of play, with a motion suitable for extremely fast movements, adaptation to differing styles of opponent competition, shot execution on the run, and with a fundamental soundness that remained steadfast under the pressures of high competition.

GRIP

The first thing anyone must know about the forehand drive is how to hold the racket properly, for it is the grip that directly determines the angle of the racket face when it contacts the ball. I advocate the use of the Eastern grip on the forehand as illustrated in the photographs below. Note that there are two bevels on the racket handle and that the "V" in one's hand, between the thumb and first finger, is located on the right bevel. This grip is sometimes referred to as the *shake-hands grip*, because of the striking similarity between it and the grip attained when one literally shakes hands with the racket. The important thing to note when studying this grip is that the wrist is in a position of strength *behind* the racket. The wrist must be kept firm in tennis, since excess movement and flexibility contribute to erratic and unpredictable shotmaking.

READY POSITION

Learning the correct ready position is very important to any stroke, for it is from this position that one leads to and from every shot on the tennis court. Note in the photograph below that the knees are bent, the legs are a comfortable distance apart, and

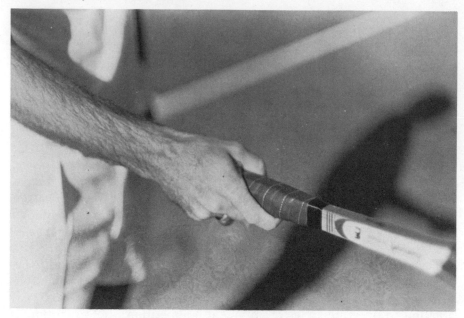

The Eastern forehand grip.

the weight is resting on the inside of the feet. From this body position, one can move quickly and decisively in any direction. The racket rests in the left hand, with the racket head held shoulder high, in a position noticeably above the level of the wrist. The left hand not only aids in supporting the racket, but facilitates quick movement when changing grips as well. One need only to loosen the grip of the right hand while turning the racket to the desired grip with the left. It is very cumbersome and highly impractical to hold the racket in the left hand and change grips by fumbling with the right.

THE SWING

Before the tennis player can begin his stroke, he must get into proper position to execute his shot, and this position is sideways, perpendicular to the net. Having maintained the ready position of the arms with the racket head still decidedly above the wrist, the player should be looking over his left shoulder as he watches the ball approach. One can arrive in this position most effectively by pivoting the shoulders from the waist and right foot. The feet do not move during the pivot; rather, they remain stationary, with rotation from the waist and shoulders being the primary source of movement. From this position, the racket is carried back shoulder high,

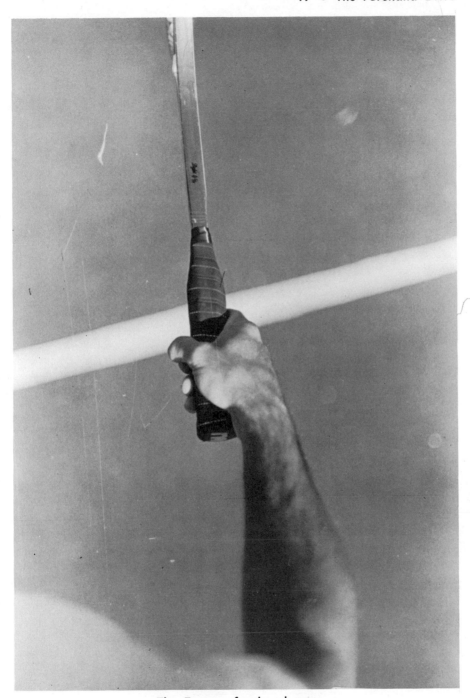

The Eastern forehand grip.

The classic ready position.

The pivot position of the forehand drive. Note shoulder coil.

In this photo the racket is parallel to the ground, the left hand is extended for balance, and the weight of the body is firmly on the left foot.

a move that arcs the shoulders inward, thereby creating a coiling action into the ball, similar in theory to the striking coil of a snake. At this time the left hand, which had been supporting the racket head, is extended toward the net, a move that serves to counterbalance the weight of the racket as it enters the backswing. At this point the racket is lowered to a position approximately parallel to the ground. This action does require some rotation in the wrist and it is through this portion of the swing that the momentum of the racket head begins to accelerate. As the racket head comes forward toward impact with the ball, a step with the left foot should be taken. This move serves to shift one's body weight into the ball, thereby allowing the player to execute the shot with considerably less effort. Learning to step with the swing is particularly useful since it instills even to the beginner the sensation of hitting on the move. The ability to do this successfully is critical if one is ever to play high-level tournament tennis. As one steps with the left foot and as the positive force of the racket proceeds forward, the player must remain in balance in order to maintain control of the shot. It is impractical and a common error to allow the right foot to be pulled around by the forward motion of the swing, since such a move would necessarily have the secondary effect of misaligning the position of the shoulders. It is similarly impractical to retain the right foot flat on the ground since the momentum of the racket would be retarded, consequently negating much of the value otherwise to be gained from stepping into the ball. The solution to this problem is rather simple and is done naturally by many players. When one drags the right foot in the latter stages of the swing, especially during the follow-through, balance is maintained and the forward motion of the racket not impaired. A drag of this type gives way and acknowledges the forward pull on the body, while at the same time retarding the excess undesirable shoulder movement that results when a player loses control of the trailing leg.

One's swing does not end with impact with the ball, for the portion of the swing known as the follow-through guides the ball and acts as the player's primary agent of control. It is useful for many to think in terms of letting the racket head follow the ball across the net, an act that insures that the finish of the stroke be extended in the front. After the arm is outstretched, the racket head should curl at the top and come to rest back in the left hand, a move that brings the player back to the original ready position, in comfortable preparation for the next shot.

This photo illustrates proper footwork, the use of the left hand for balance, as well as excellent concentration.

A fine example of how balance is maintained through the efficient use of right-foot drag.

Proper follow-through extension is always in front, back to the left hand.

2
THE BACKHAND DRIVE

The backhand drive is a stumbling block for many beginners, and is often a weakness to be exploited until mastered. It is a shot to which much pressure will always be directed until a definite stand is taken and demonstration of a basic backhand adequacy illustrated. Those players who have developed the backhand as their dominant side include the immortal Australian Ken Rosewall, the very aggressive topspin drives of Ilie Nastase and Grand Slam winners Rod Laver and Don Budge, as well as the fluid execution developed by Maureen Connoly, Billie Jean King, and the young Wimbledon winner Evonne Goolagong.

GRIP

Use of the proper grips is fundamental in the development of any sound stroke. The Eastern grips are the most widely used today and it is these that this book recommends. In the photograph of the Eastern backhand below, note the position of the hand in relation to the two bevels on the handle. This grip is a quarter of a turn to the left of the Eastern forehand, and is attained when the "V" in the hand (between the thumb and first finger) comes to rest on the left bevel. This grip puts the wrist in a position of strength behind the racket, consequently allowing the player to execute his stroke with a firm wrist as the racket impacts with the ball. A word of caution, however, since this should not be misinterpreted to mean that the wrist should be kept completely rigid throughout the entire swing. The development of a fluid swing, as set forth in this book, necessitates the use of a controlled amount of wrist rotation as the racket head gains momentum in the back part of the semielliptical swing. Likewise, rotation should not be confused with flexibility, since the controlled swing of rhythm and balance is possible with neither extreme rigidity nor flexibility.

The Eastern backhand grip.

READY POSITION

When executing the backhand, one leads into, from, and finishes toward the same basic ready position discussed previously with respect to the forehand. The knees should be bent, racket held shoulder high, with the body weight distributed on the inside of the feet. Such a position facilitates quick movement to and from the stroke, supports the weight of the racket head and keeps it above wrist level, and is a position from which the player can change grips with a minimum amount of effort.

THE SWING

When learning the groundstrokes, it is useful to view the backhand as a twin to the forehand. By doing this, and by executing the two strokes with a fundamental likeness, one lends a unique quality of continuity to the backcourt game that becomes invaluable as one progresses toward tournament level competition.

The forehand drive discussed earlier began with a pivot from the right foot. In the same way, the backhand for right handed player begins with a pivot from the left foot. The feet do not move during this portion of the swing; rather the shoulders and waist are the primary source of rotation once the player has reached the ball. He

The pivot position of the backhand drive. Note the shoulder coil.

A fine example of hitting on the move, body weight into the ball, left-hand balance.

should be sideways, perpendicular to the net, watching the ball approach over the right shoulder. In this position, the shoulders have arched inward, again assuming the coiling position of strength. The spring action of the coil unfolds as the racket is lowered in the back with the left hand. Extension of the left hand in the back, as the racket proceeds forward, insures good balance throughout the shot, by serving to counterbalance the positive force of the racket as it accelerates into the ball. Getting the racket head *down in the back*, with the racket closely paralleling the ground, is critical to proper execution of this swing, since it is through this segment of the motion that the racket head gains momentum. As the racket nears impact with the ball, a step with the right foot should be taken in order to shift the body weight into the ball, thus eliminating the use of the energy, otherwise necessary to be spent by the arm. It allows the weight of the body and the momentum of the racket to work for the player, rather than as an obstacle to be overcome. The trailing left foot should drag during the later stages of the swing, in order to insure adequate balance during the stroke. This is especially useful when one is pulled badly out of position where good balance is essential to a controlled return. The drag serves to acknowledge

Well-balanced execution, with the weight of the body firmly planted on the right foot, racket parallel to the ground, good concentration, eyes on the ball.

Well-balanced execution of the difficult high backhand. Again it is possible to note efficient use of left-foot drag.

The follow through of the backhand drive. Note the extension of the finish and the balancing action of the left hand.

the forward motion of the swing, while at the same time retarding any excess movement that might otherwise misalign the shoulders. The backhand is finished by following through toward the net in the same manner described with respect to the forehand. In spite of the fact that the ball has already been contacted, it is, nevertheless, the followthrough that guides the ball toward its destination and lends control to the shot. A fact of such magnitude should not be readily forgotten.

3
THE SERVICE

A player serves half of the games played in a tennis match, a fact
that is conceded by most to make the serve the most important
stroke in the game. Any stroke that is good enough to give a player
a distinctive advantage fifty percent of the time must be considered
an undeniable asset. It is notable, also, that this is the only stroke
over which one always retains complete control. In all other circumstances on the court a man is responsible for playing any ball within the playing area, and is totally dependent on how and where the
opponent might direct the ball. As would be the case with a shot
of such importance, it remains very elusive and difficult to master.
No one learns an attacking service easily, for it is a shot that requires
dedicated practice and the willingness to hit hundreds of balls, often alone, when a less intensive practice with a companion might
seem more enjoyable. Rote practice, training the body for an ab-
stract goal—the development of a fluid Gonzalez, Kramer, Laver,
Goolagong, Court, King-type motion capable of imparting differing
speeds, twists, and slices to the ball—is all part of the intangible dream of the inspired tennis player.

GRIP

The grip one uses while serving directly affects the angle of the
racket face when it contacts the ball, and is the primary determi-
nant of the amount and type of spin imparted to the serve. Note
in the photograph the angle of the racket face and how it increases
as one progresses from the Western to Eastern backhand grip. The
Western grip is all but obsolete today and its use is not recommended in this book. The Eastern forehand is the most comfortable for
the beginning player, since use of this grip allows the racket to contact the ball nearly flush, with very little angle with relation to the
ball. As one progresses and masters the basic service motion, the use
of spin becomes most desirable. Many pros and coaches recommend
the Continental grip when serving. This grip is illustrated above also, and is found by resting the hand in a position between the East-

| Western | Eastern Forehand | Continental | Eastern Backhand |

ern forehand and backhand. There are some players who prefer not to change grips in their ground game and it is this grip that they use. When serving spin, however, I have found it most desirable to use the Eastern backhand, a grip that gives as much natural angle on the racket face as possible. This angle on the racket face causes the racket to graze or brush the edge of the ball, consequently making the ball spin. Because of the initial difficulty of changing from the Eastern forehand to backhand when learning spin serves, many players find it useful to change in progression to the Continental, and then to the Eastern backhand, since the Continental grip is an intermediary grip between the two.

Just as there was a necessary ready position for the ground strokes, there is a similar need to assume some established position before one begins to serve. This position, as illustrated below, finds the right foot parallel to the baseline and the left foot at approximately a forty-five-degree angle. The ultimate problem of service placement is solved from this position, since any movement of the right foot also changes the relative position of the shoulders. Any time the shoulder position changes so does the swing and, consequently, the direction of the ball. The proper positions of the feet for placement to the four corners of the service court are listed below.

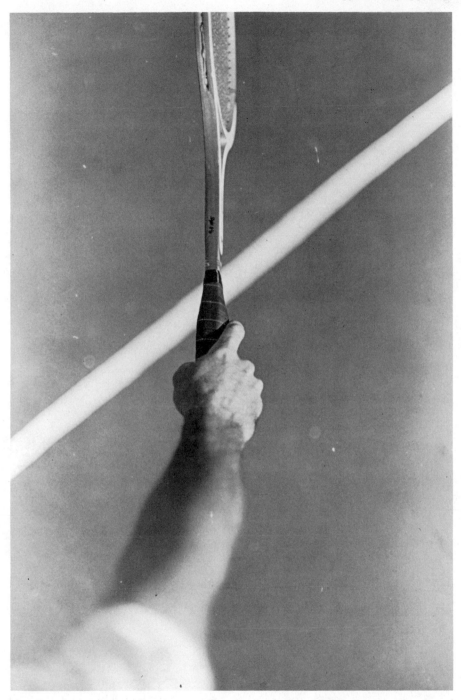

The Continental grip: an intermediary grip between the Eastern forehand and backhand.

The service ready position with the weight of the body resting on the back (right) foot.

FOOT POSITION

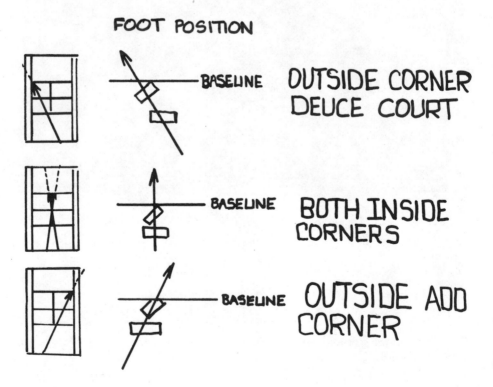

BASELINE — **OUTSIDE CORNER DEUCE COURT**

BASELINE — **BOTH INSIDE CORNERS**

BASELINE — **OUTSIDE ADD CORNER**

THE SWING

The first thing one must do in serving, after assuming the ready position just described, is relax the arms, focus on a spot in the desired service court, and begin allowing the racket to drop, naturally, letting the racket head become the primary source of momentum. This portion of the swing should be unhurried and rhythmic, in an action similar to the swinging pendulum of a clock. The left arm should be tossing the ball simultaneously, thus allowing both arms to work together in unison. The toss is a very critical element of the service motion since, in essence, it is the only variable in the stroke. Control of the toss can make the unorthodox swing appear consistent, just as the bad toss can often make the fundamentally correct motion appear ineffective and uncontrolled. Note in the photograph, that the proper toss begins with the ball resting in three fingers of the hand. It is not advisable to toss the ball from the palm of the hand, since the ball is likely to roll out of the hand, becoming erratic and inconsistent. The controlled toss is deliberately placed to the height of racket extension at impact, with the left arm remaining extended in a follow-through type action. The follow-through of the service toss leaves the left arm extended after the ball has left the hand until the forward swing of the right arm brings the racket and body momentum into the ball.

As the ball is being tossed, the right arm should be raised to a position approximately parallel to the ground. At this time the arm is bent and tucked into a throwing position that closely parallels the football or baseball player as he draws his throwing arm back. The exact place in the swing that this tuck begins always varies slightly and should take place wherever the player feels most comfortable. The arm and racket are distinctly BEHIND the head, in this position, in order to employ the use of the very strong muscles of the back. The action of the racket whips behind the player, forming a loop that is again conducive to racket-head momentum and acceleration. The player should stretch high as the racket nears impact with the ball in order to gain maximum angle down into the service court. After contact with the ball, the followthrough should bring the racket across the body to the left side.

The unhurried and rhythmic pendulum swing that begins the service motion.

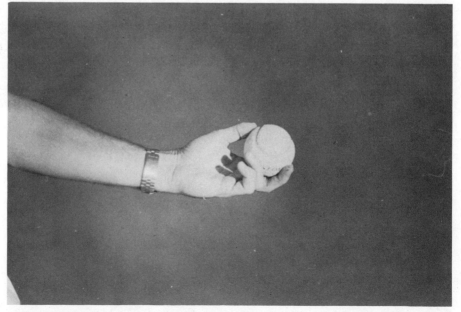

A controlled toss is best attained by allowing the ball to rest in three fingers of the hand.

Toss and the end of the pendulum swing.

Toss follow through and right-arm tuck.

Toss follow through drops as player enters extension and impact with the ball.

WEIGHT TRANSFER AND THE COILING ACTION OF THE SERVE

The generation of power in the service is not an assimilation of brute strength; rather it is the tangible result of a highly coordinated transfer of weight coupled with the coiling spring action of the entire body. Such a motion is the culmination of a highly diversified muscular action involving the legs, back, shoulders, arms, and wrist. Coordination and integration of these bodily parts is essential in order to insure the ultimate success of championship level service.

As one assumes the ready position for serving, the body weight should be stationed on the right foot. From this position, all body action will be directed forward, into the ball and toward the net. As the racket is lowered into the pendulum swing preceding the tucked throwing position, the first weight transfer occurs, from the right to left foot. In this position, the left knee should be bent, supporting the full weight of the body until the forward motion of the racket begins. Every player seeks rhythm in his strokes in order to facilitate repetition of a constant stroke type, and this is commonly attained during this knee bend. It is from this position that the spring action of the bodily coil is unleashed and the body weight transferred into the ball. This important body action is combined with the accumulated momentum of the racket behind the head to insure a maximum force at the moment of impact. The motion finishes with the followthrough as the player allows his weight to be shifted back to the right foot as it is carried naturally into the court by the forward pull of the swing.

THE CANNONBALL (FLAT) SERVICE

The primary advantage of the Cannonball service lies in the player's ability to hit the ball very hard. Pancho Gonzalez is more famous than any for the development of this serve but others such as John Newcomb, Arthur Ashe, and Stan Smith have also developed the elusive combination of speed and control necessary for mastery of this shot. Because of its lack of spin, which often lends control, this serve must also be considered one of the more difficult shots to serve consistently. Many players use the Eastern forehand grip with this service, since there is very little angle created on the racket face, consequently allowing the racket to contact the ball as flatly as possible. It is possible to serve the ball flat using a Continental or Eastern backhand grip, however, but these positions require turning the wrist inward in order to compensate for the angle naturally created by these grips. The toss is the primary variable in any service motion and it is the placement of the toss that combines with

The first transfer of weight is from the right to left foot and occurs as the player executes the tuck and toss of the motion.

The release of the body coil. At this point the full thrust of the body is directed into the ball.

The forward motion of the swing pulling the right leg across after impact.

The completed follow through.

the grip to impart spin, or the lack of it, to the ball. When serving a flat serve, the toss should be placed directly over the head and slightly in front, allowing one to shift the full weight of the body into the ball. As mentioned before, weight transfer and an effective coiling action are the primary source of strength in serving. Strength, power, and pace are the chief characteristics of the flat serve, and they are enhanced to the fullest when this portion of the motion is executed properly. A serve of this type is most wisely used as a first serve since the percentage of accuracy is rather low because of the lack of spin, and not sufficient to warrant the chance of a double fault. Double faulting in tennis must be considered all but unforgivable, especially in tournament level play where winning the service games is so critical.

THE SLICE SERVICE

While the Slice service is usually the first spin serve the beginning player learns, it is also one used even by world-class competitors in the highest competition. Its use has been made famous by such serving artists as Jack Kramer, Arthur Ashe, and Rod Laver. Of its predominant assets to the intermediate player is the fact that the spin lends control to the ball, consequently making it very suitable as a second serve. The Slice serve is attained by using the Continental or Eastern backhand grip, and by tossing the ball to the right. This combination allows the player to contact the ball on its right side, and therefore impart a spin that curves the ball to the left in its flight and induce a slide left after the bounce. The execution of the basic service motion when serving a Slice serve does not change, the only variables being the grip and toss. It is a fact that spin slows the ball down, but it is important to note the common misconception that this slower pace is the result of a slower swing. Spin serves are slower and more controlled because only an edge of the ball actually contacts the racket, as well as the additional fact that much of the force applied by the racket is absorbed by the turning ball.

THE TOPSPIN SERVICE

The Topspin service is a very versatile serve and can be used as a first or second delivery, as illustrated by the legendary serving of Lew Hoad, Tony Trabert, Roy Emerson, and again, Rod Laver. This diversity derives from the fact that the topspin has the dual effect of assuring an aggressive bounce forward, while enjoying the desirable effect the spin has of pulling the ball down into the service court. Topspin turns the ball straight over, exactly as its name im-

The Cannonball service. Note the tuck of the right arm, the coiling action, and the position of the toss.

The slice service. Note the position of the toss to the right.

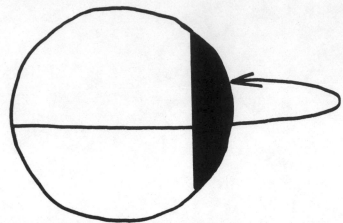

THE SLICE SERVICE CONTACTS THE
BALL ON ITS RIGHT SIDE, INDUCING
IT TO CURVE TO THE LEFT

THE TOPSPIN SERVICE BRUSHES
THE BALL ON ITS BACK SIDE AND
TURNS IT STRAIGHT OVER

plies, and is attained by brushing up the back side of the ball. The service toss must, therefore, be placed over the player's head to the left, so as to allow the racket to come *over* the ball, rather than to its side as witnessed in the Slice. The Eastern backhand grip becomes more of a necessity as one progresses to the Topspin and Twist serves, the toss of which is to the left, over one's head. Note in the photo the arched back that is necessary in order to reach such a toss. Other than this slight variation, the basic motion of the serve remains the same, with the action of the unfolding coil being fundamental to all, regardless of the type of serve being used.

THE AMERICAN TWIST SERVICE

The American Twist service is the most difficult spin serve to learn because of its peculiar combination of top and side spin. Those who have demonstrated mastery of this difficult shot include Lew Hoad, Tony Trabert, John Newcomb, and Rod Laver. Use of the wrist is necessary to attain this difficult combination of spins, and is accomplished by effectively brushing over the ball at a diagonal from left to right. As was the case with the Topspin serve, it is necessary to arch the back in order to reach the toss placed over the player's head. The American Twist is a heavily spin-laden serve that hangs in the air considerably longer than any other serve, with the excess spin causing the ball to arc over the net by a very safe margin before being effected by the eventual down-pull of the rapid overspin. This fact not only lends itself well to the player seeking more time to reach good volleying position at the net but serves to make it a very desirable second serve as well. The erratic, and therefore very aggressive, kick that follows the bounce has the positive effect of putting the receiver in the precarious position of returning a very unpredictable high bouncing ball. This is an invaluable service for the player aspiring to play high-level tournament tennis. In view of the current boom in tennis, competition has stiffened, with all of the relative competency levels having been undeniably upgraded. The tournament player today must be the master of all of the serves just described. He must have the ability to direct changing speeds and spins to any of the four corners at will, always changing and alternating the serves, to avoid the establishment of predictable patterns of play.

The topspin service. As the player uncoils, he will brush up and over the back side of the ball.

THE AMERICAN TWIST SERVE IS
CHARACTERIZED BY A RATHER PECULIAR
COMBINATION OF TOP AND SIDE SPIN

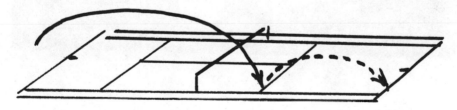

THE HIGH ARCH AND FORWARD KICK
OF THE AMERICAN TWIST SERVICE

The American twist service. Note the toss over the player's head, the arched back, and the full extension of the toes.

4

THE VOLLEY

The term *volley* is used with reference to any ball hit before the bounce, and for this reason is usually executed from a position near the net. In the fast and aggressive games played today, the ability to play the net effectively has become all but essential. There is considerable advantage to hitting the ball from a position close to the net, since it allows the player to cut off the opponent's return before it reaches its full angle. It successfully cuts short the time available to an opponent to retrieve the ball but inherently limits the time available to the man executing the shot as well. These relative advantages and disadvantages must always be weighed against one another and reflected in both the technique a player uses in executing his shot as well as in his tactical strategy that ultimately determines when and where he attempts the shot.

CONTINENTAL VERSUS EASTERN GRIPS: THE GRIP DEBATE FOR PLAY AT THE NET

There is considerable controversy today concerning the pros and cons of different grips used at the net, with some debating whether there is sufficient time to make any change at all. Many proponents of the latter make the mistake of viewing the elements of the swing in sequential segments, an argument that refutes itself when one accepts the fact that more than a single bodily movement can be executed at the same time. It is my opinion that a player's grip can be changed in the same move that the player takes his racket back. I do not, however, discourage players from using the Continental grip, which eliminates the problem of grip changes, at the net or elsewhere. It is a legitimate grip and one that fits the needs of many players very well. I have found that students need latitude to develop naturally; consequently, I am inclined to leave this decision up to the player until an obvious inadequacy or lack of strength in the wrist is displayed. If such a weakness occurs, I encourage use of the Eastern grips, again since their position more behind the racket lends added support, thereby offering compensation for a natural deficiency of this type.

THE FOREHAND VOLLEY

The development of an aggressive and consistent volley is essential in tournament-level competition, in order to follow the aggressive sequence of the contemporary serve-and-volley game. Those players noted for their highly efficient play at the net, on the forehand side, include Australians Frank Sedgman, Rod Laver, and Margaret Court, and Americans Pancho Gonzalez, Jack Kramer, Arthur Ashe, and Billie Jean King. All of these great champions have executed the forehand volley decisively and in the manner advocated by this author.

The forehand volley begins from the classic ready position, knees bent with the racket held shoulder high in the left hand. The first move out of this position requires getting into hitting position, again sideways and perpendicular to the net. The racket is taken back as far as the right shoulder, where it is cut short, thus forming what is commonly known as a *punch* stroke for play at the net. The racket head should be kept above wrist level in this stroke, and it is most effectively controlled when the path of the swing is directed diagonally, chipping the ball, with the backspin serving as a very useful agent of control. When volleying below the level of the net, the swing is even shorter, with the racket face open, thereby allowing the ball to be projected over the net via the pace applied by the opponent's oncoming shot. A step forward with the left foot should be taken simultaneously with this action in order to maintain the closed body position with the shoulders sideways to net, so as to insure a steadfast position that doesn't vary from shot to shot. Stepping with the left foot in this case, then, does not parallel the need to shift the body weight forward as seen in the groundstrokes. The volley, instead, attains its aggressive effect from the fact that the netman's position closer to the net, severely reduces the time available for the opponent to react. Additionally, stepping with the right foot forces the player to hit from an open-shoulder stance, a fact that contributes to the ultimate loss of at least a full step in potential reach. This is a significant point since a player has only a given amount of time to make his shot and always seeks to cover the court in the most economical way possible. The volley is a *touch* shot where one seeks to manipulate the opposition into areas of vulnerability that eventually lead to player downfall. The serve and volley game is aggressive because of the overall effect of the shot pattern, serve followed by volley, and not because any one shot is completely overwhelming.

THE BACKHAND VOLLEY

Complete playing adequacy at the net necessitates the develop-

This is a very decisive forehand volley, with the full weight of the body being directed into the ball. Note the step with the left foot toward the net.

The pivot position of the forehand volley.

The low forehand volley. Note the open racket face, left-hand balance, and proper footwork.

ment of a decisive backhand volley. Those players exemplifying the highly efficient and aggressive execution necessary to compete in world class competition include the great Australians Ken Rosewall, Lew Hoad, Rod Laver, Margaret Court and Evonne Goolagong and Americans Billie Jean King, Tony Trabert, Pancho Gonzalez, and Stan Smith, all of whom play the shot with authority and complete confidence. Their execution is noteworthy because of their consistently decisive effect, which arises directly from the sound and concise method employed.

There is a basic continuity to the volley, elements that remain the same for its execution on both the forehand and backhand sides. Of these, *proper footwork* and a *shortened swing* are the most prominent. As with the forehand, the first move into the stroke begins with the pivot, getting the player into proper hitting position. This does not involve movement of the feet; rather, it is a rotation from the waist and shoulders. This move is not as pronounced as it is with ground stroke execution and often occurs only a split second before the step and swing. Shifting the body weight into the ball is directly related to proper footwork, and occurs as the player steps into the ball, simultaneous with his swing. It is very important that this step be taken with the right foot, since stepping with the left, when retrieving a ball to the left side necessarily misaligns the shoulder position that is so critical to the execution of a successful shot. An

The pivot position of the backhand volley.

error in footwork that leaves the shoulders facing the net is called an *open stance* and is not recommended. As mentioned before, a step with the incorrect foot loses the player at least one step, a critical fact since, during most exchanges at the net, there is time for only one. The step one takes, therefore, should afford the player as much ground as possible. The swing is short, a punch stroke that originates primarily from the right shoulder. The muscles of the arm are taut, but the elbow is not locked. The player should lean on the shoulder, directing the ball with a straight arm and a diagonal swing, imparting a controlled amount of backspin. Chipping the ball in this manner slows the ball down, lending control and consistency. Hitting with a straight arm is advisable here because it eliminates the potential variable that occurs with flexibility in the elbow. Additionally, the racket head should be kept above the level of the wrist, since the wrist is also a source of unwanted flexibility. Note in the photo how the wrist is firm and the racket in a position paralleling the ground. The swing on the low volley is very short, the ball being propelled from the pace on the opponent's oncoming ball, and being directed over the net via the open position of the racket face. This theory of using the applied force of the opponent's shot, by using an abbreviated swing and an open racket face, underlies all shots played at the net, but is exemplified most clearly during the execution of the low volley.

The low backhand volley. Note that the knees are bent, racket face open, and left hand extended for balance.

5

THE OVERHEAD SMASH

The overhead smash is almost exclusively mastered among players of world-class ability, rarely is missed, and most often serves to end the point in a single attempt. Those players noteworthy for their ability to cover even the best lobs include the Australian Rod Laver and Americans Pancho Gonzalez, Stan Smith, and Jack Kramer. These players hit the overhead smash decisively with very precise placement, while using sound and concise execution.

The development of a consistent and decisive overhead smash, of the type just described, is essential in order to compete successfully in tournament-level tennis today. Fast and aggressive games are played with players spending as much time at the net as possible. There is more shot making, pinpoint placement, and flair for the spectacular than ever before. But it is in this context that it is possible to witness players losing games and even matches because of their inability to conclude the point when their opponent resorts to the defensive tactic of lobbing. Such a void in an aggressive player's game is most unfortunate since, theoretically, the difficult part of the sequence has been completed once the opposition is forced into the use of such a tactic. Because of this rather widespread deficiency, especially among junior-level players, many have found the development of a sound defense to be a good offense, and a formula for winning matches. This tactic is short-lived as a winning strategy, however, once the aggressive player equips his arsenal of shots with a sound overhead to support and reinforce his net game.

THE BASIC MOTION

Close observation has revealed that the critical element of the overhead smash is getting under the ball. This thought directly parallels the previous discussion of the serve and how an erratic toss can contribute to inconsistent serving. The player faces a comparable problem with the overhead since, when he fails to get in proper position under the ball, he is forced to make some physical deviation in his swing. Thus, as soon as the lob is recognized, the play-

The body weight is planted on the right foot as the player retreats and enters the abbreviated swing of the overhead smash. Note left-hand extension paralleling the motion of the serve.

er should, first and foremost, position himself correctly, sideways to the net and under the ball. At this point, the player should enter an abbreviated service swing, taking the racket back to the tuck position without the intermediary drop of the racket into the pendulum swing discussed with respect to the serve. In the same move, the left hand is raised, paralleling the action of the service toss, and acting as an aiming device and reference agent for correct body position under the ball.

The footwork and shift in body weight *does not* parallel the serve. As one retreats under the ball, via a sidestepping run, the racket is tucked in the back and the right foot planted. In the serve, the body weight has already been shifted from the right to left foot by the time this tuck occurs. The body coils despite this apparent difference and the knees bend. In the overhead, the right foot crosses to a lesser degree after the swing and there is less followthrough. The right foot follows more naturally on the service since all weight transfer is forward, into the ball and toward the net, in preparation for good volleying position. The very nature of the overhead forces the player to retreat backward, after which he must plant the right foot and redirect his body weight forward, back into the ball.

THE SCISSOR KICK

There are times that every netman is caught by surprise by the lob. In these cases, as well as when placement of the lob is exceptionally deep, it becomes impossible to reach an ideal position directly under the ball. It is under these circumstances that many players execute the overhead by jumping in a technique commonly referred to as a *scissor kick*. It is commonly used on the tournament level of tennis, since at this level lobs are often very accurate. It is best to retreat toward the kick via the same sidestepping run that was discussed with respect to the basic overhead motion. A move of this type allows the player to keep his eye on the ball while moving in the fastest way possible. The weight of the body is planted on the right foot, after which the player pushes off, springing into the kick as he begins the shot. The player maintains his balance during the shot by throwing the right leg forward counterbalancing the forward motion of the swing. The player lands on his left foot first, after which the basic ready position is again assumed in preparation for the next shot.

The side-stepping run used as the player retreats into proper position under the lob.

The scissor kick.

The player lands on the left foot after the scissor kick.

6
THE LOB

The lob is one of the most maligned and underrated shots in the game of tennis. It is not a shot used exclusively as a last resort and need not always be defensive in nature. When used wisely, it can change the pace of the game, keep the overanxious netman constantly on his guard, as well as serving as an excellent response when pulled badly out of position. There is no set technique for the lob since it is executed off of the fundamental forehand and backhand ground strokes and is often hit in awkward positions on the run. It is important, however, that an aggressive lob be well disguised and made to look as much like one's normal swing as possible. If this is done effectively, the opponent is forced to react to the ball after it is in the air, consequently negating any advantage to be gained from

A lob effectively used against a netman crowding the net too close.

early anticipation. It has often been said that deception is a subtle but very sophisticated art, whether it be practiced in actual warfare, over the chess board, or on the tennis court; and such a statement is certainly applicable here.

THE DEFENSIVE LOB

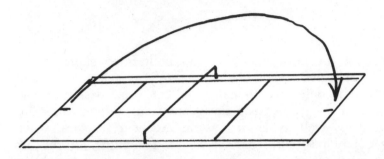

THE HIGH ARCH OF THE DEFENSIVE LOB

The arc of the defensive lob is characterized by its height, and is illustrated in the diagram above. This shot is hit high and deep in order to give the player a maximum amount of time to recover and get back into good position for the next shot. It is very important that the ball be kept deep, since the short lob is readily put away. There are very few players who will consistently put the ball away from the baseline and it is for this reason that a defensive lob is a tactic often used to negate an advantage gained by the opponent in a preceding part of the sequence.

THE CHIPPED LOB

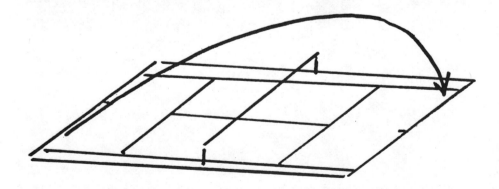

THE CONTROLLED CHIPPED LOB

The chipped lob is less defensive than the lob type just described and it is necessary that the player be in better position, in order to hit a controlled shot. It is lower and reaches its destination sooner, thereby rushing the opponent's return and making it more difficult. The backspin on the ball slows the shot down, and it should be noted that its excessive use will cause the ball to hang. Neither of these characteristics can be viewed as desirable since the object of the shot is to get the ball over the opponent's head as soon as possible, thereby cutting down the time the opponent has to react and make an adequate return. The second liability of this shot arises from the fact that the chipped lob can usually be detected by the low follow-through that accompanies it. The degree to which this characteristic exists always varies with the individual. If there is a noticeable difference between the player's normal stroke and the way he chips his lob, early anticipation is likely to occur, detracting much from the effectiveness of the shot. The chipped lob is most effectively used by the player who uses the spin factor as a means of additional control, while deceiving his opponent with clever body fakes from the shoulders, head, and eyes.

THE TOPSPIN LOB

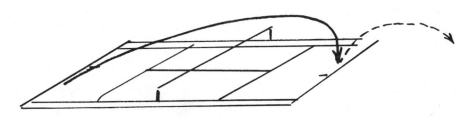

THE TOPSPIN LOB

The topspin lob is only witnessed on the higher levels of play and must be considered one of the more difficult and spectacular shots in the game. It is extremely difficult to anticipate since, in essence, it is but a high topspin drive, with the excessive spin acting to pull the ball into the court. The swing does not appear as premeditated as the more deliberate chipped lob, with the speed of the racket head necessarily being fast in order to lift the ball. The opponent is seldom able to anticipate the topspin lob because of the striking similarity of appearance to that of the ground strokes. It is a very aggressive shot and is executed most effectively when the player is in good position, with passing shot options at his disposal as well. The ball kicks forward after the bounce, making play after it bounces very difficult. If the shot is undetected by the time it passes over the netman's head, it will more than likely be successful even against the fastest opponents. The topspin lob has been used with a large degree of success by the former Wimbledon champion, American Chuck McKinley, as well as by the flamboyant 1972 U. S. Open winner from Romania, Ilie Nastase.

Part II.   Strategy and Tactics: Aggressive Player Initiatives and Selected Defensive Responses

"Experienced players gradually learn all of the possible angles of attack just as the billiard player must know by rote every natural angle of the billiard table. There are just so many possibilities of danger from any given position, and the expert is familiar with them all."[1]

Tennis has much in common with chess. Most important, the opening move is visualized as a premeditated series of steps leading to a quick and decisive advantage over an opponent. In today's fast and aggressive games, a point may be completed within three or four exchanges; consequently, the competent player should be aware of potential strategy at least this far ahead, calculating his opponent's weaknesses, not just in terms of single faulty strokes, but in terms of larger patterns of strategic error. The opening service is a tip-off for the anticipated sequence of events, including probable defensive responses. Behind the lightning quick responses of the professional is a thinking man whose mind is always several steps ahead of his physical responses.

The purpose of this section is to define the aggressive player's opening options as planned sets of initiatives. Common defensive responses to these initiatives are then noted, beginning with the ones that are powerful enough to reverse the course of the game. In all cases, the player behaviors are shown pictorially, as well as described in the narrative text. The chapters that follow are designated by the type of initial service—Cannonball, Slice and Topspin and American Twist. In each case, the analysis follows the intended placement of the ball:

1. Outside corner deuce court
2. Inside corner deuce court
3. Inside corner add court
4. Outside corner add court

The text is technical but no more so than the actual game. The reader will find the material organized in such a way as to permit selective study and/or review of a particular strategy, irrespective of its sequencing in the chapter.

1. J. Parmley Paret, *Psychology and Advanced Play*, Vol. III. The Lawn Tennis Library, American Lawn Tennis Inc., New York: 1927, p. 35.

7

THE CANNONBALL (FLAT) SERVICE

OUTSIDE-CORNER DEUCE COURT

The Cannonball service is characterized by its excessive speed and has been exemplified by such players as Pancho Gonzalez, Stan Smith, John Newcomb and Arthur Ashe. This serve is difficult to control

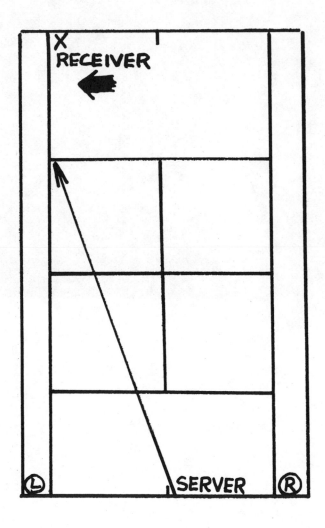

because of its lack of spin, and is mastered only on the highest levels of play. Many players are able to hit the serve very hard, but relatively few are capable of the pinpoint placement achieved by these great champions. Without this placement and variety, the speed already on the ball can often be used to propel the return back over the net. Thus, it is because of the excessive speed on both the serve and its blocked return that it is not uncommon to see the server caught in the precarious position of volleying from his shoe tops in *no-man's land* (that area of the court between the baseline and proper volleying position inside the service line). This happens when the player fails to acknowledge control as a priority and seeks only to overwhelm his opponent with excessive speed. With proper placement and variety, however, this service can be one of the most awesome weapons at a player's disposal, and it is in this light that it will be treated.

The flat serve to the outside corner of the deuce court has the advantage of crossing the diagonal of the service court, a fact that allows a maximum margin for error. The distance from the server to impact point is always longest to the outside corners. The server is also aided by the fact that the receiver is led away from the cen-

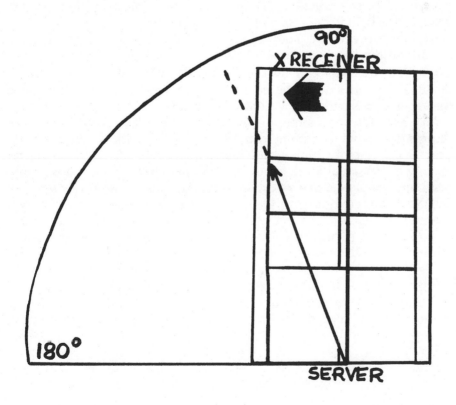

ter of the court, thus creating an area of vulnerability for the server's next shot to the right. The angle of the serve increases the further the receiver is pulled off of the court. Couple these facts with the excessive speed of this serve and the likelihood of an aggressive response becomes small indeed. This speed factor makes it very difficult to receive the Cannonball serve unless it can be done with reflex action alone. If the ball is so placed that any number of steps are necessary to retrieve it, the server will retain the initiative the majority of the time.

Because of the fact that the time required to reach the net is shortened from the fast pace of the serve, it is of utmost importance that the server incorporate a definite forward motion toward the net into his service swing and follow-through. The players that follow the Cannonball service to the net wisely incorporate this action into their service motion, at times saving as much as three full steps. Exactly how much ground is saved, of course, is relative and directly dependent on the natural speed of the player in question and how adept he is in compensating for a deficiency of this type.

The server rushing the net is wise to employ use of the potential percentage angle concept by dissecting the angle of the receiver's return of serve. Raymond Little defined the concept well when he stated in *Tennis Tactics,* "There is an ever moving angle whose head is the ball at the moment of impact with the racket, and whose sides are the extreme lines of flight which the ball may take and remain within the boundaries of the court. The proper defensive position is in the center of this angle—not in the center of the court."[1] Shading the left side of the court is particularly effective here, since the receiver's chances for a controlled return of great angle are very small. The forcing nature of the flat serve often forces defensive returns such that the point can be concluded with a single volley. This is not hard to understand when one faces the prospect of returning professional-level serves that often exceed one hundred miles per hour. If the service return is hit defensively, the server's volley should be directed deep to the right side of the court. Having drawn the receiver wide to the left with the serve, a volley deep to the right side of the court becomes the most decisive conclusion to the point. Hitting the ball deep eliminates much of the probability of play after the bounce, since the receiver has already been maneuvered wide left by the serve. If the service return is directed low, or in any manner threatening to the retainment of server initiative, the volley is most effectively placed *short* to the right side. The short volley draws

1. J. Parmley Paret, *Psychology and Advanced Play,* Vol. III. The Lawn Tennis Library, American Lawn Tennis Inc. New York: 1927, p. 94.

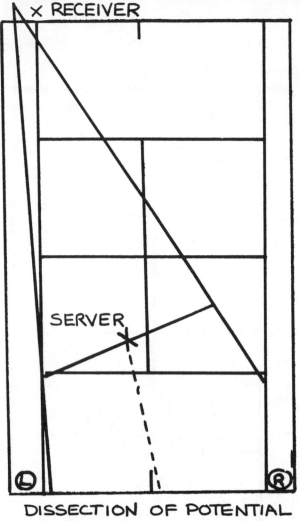

DISSECTION OF POTENTIAL PERCENTAGE ANGLE

Note how the player in the foreground has shaded left of the center service line, dissecting the potential angle of the opponent's return.

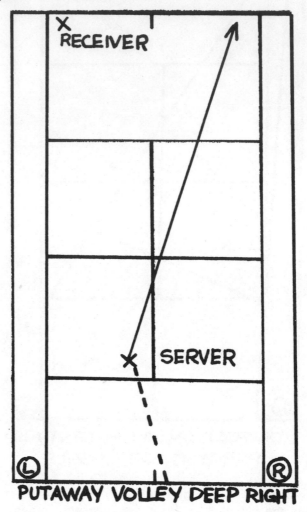

PUTAWAY VOLLEY DEEP RIGHT

the opponent inside the court, thereby putting him in a vulnerable position for a final shot behind him deep to the left. It is again wise to dissect the angle of the opponent's return, this time by shading to the right side of the court, where the first volley was directed. Because all angles widen as their arms lengthen, it is also wise to move closer to the net when positioning oneself for this second shot. Moving closer to the net quickens the pace of the game, thereby limiting the time available to the receiver to reposition himself for response to the server's second volley.

One holds a distinct advantage while serving, for the server can begin the initiative in any number of ways, all of which are unknown to the receiver until after the initiative has begun. For this reason,

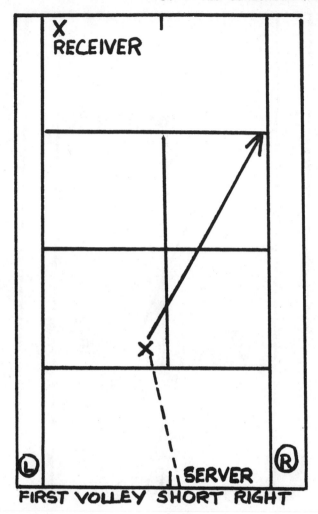

X
RECEIVER

X

Ⓛ   Ⓡ

SERVER

FIRST VOLLEY SHORT RIGHT

defensive returns or returns without purpose serve only to reinforce the strength of the position held by the server. This fact becomes more obvious the higher the caliber of play one observes. In order to break serve, the receiver must put together a series of returns good enough to reverse the original initiative set forth by the server. The critical shot in this sequence is the initial return of serve. Thus, if this shot is truly forcing, the stage is set for initiative reversal with the end of the point being imminent. How one chooses to end the point, if not already lost by a server error, will vary directly according to the court position of his defensive volley, individual receiver strengths and weaknesses, and the receivers evaluation of the server's vulnerability. Effective passing shots vary, with the topspin shots

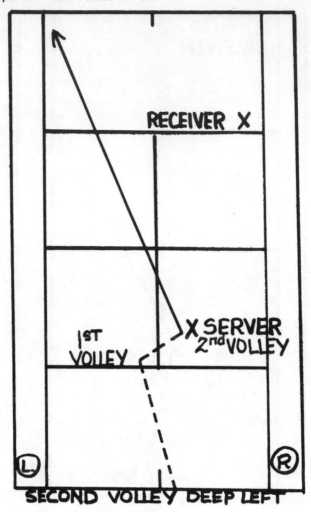

RECEIVER X

1ST VOLLEY

X SERVER 2nd VOLLEY

L ®

SECOND VOLLEY DEEP LEFT

being the most effective because of their tendency to dip below net level. Other aggressive shots used to complete the point after the original initiative has been reversed include touch shots of great angle, driving shots down either line, and lobs deep enough and high enough to be beyond the netman's reach.

Responses

The speed of the Cannonball serve can be reversed and used against the server rushing the net. In order to do this, the receiver must stand on or near the baseline when receiving. This is against the natural inclinations of most since the first reaction of many is to back away from the hard hit ball. Such a move is a distinct disadvantage to the receiver, since the angle on the serve will widen in direct relation to the length of the angle arms. In other words, the farther one moves back, the farther one also has to move to reach the ball. Attacking the ball early shortens the time available to the server to reach good volleying position at the net, since the server always has a given distance to cover in his charge of the net. Just as the excessive spin of the American Twist keeps the ball in the air longer, the inherent speed of the flat serve cuts this time short, thus pressuring the server that is not exceptionally fast. Catching

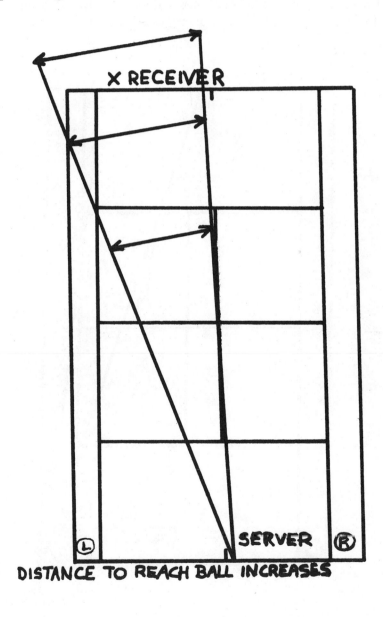

the serve early by standing near the baseline often enables the receiver to catch the netman in an awkward position in "no-man's land," between the baseline and service line.

The best return of serve from this corner is down-the-line. A return of this type is well suited to a serve of such high speed, since the direction of a ball down-the-line necessarily entails contacting the ball slightly late. It has the additional advantage of not crossing the path of the server as he follows to the net. But because of the control necessary on a shot of this nature, it must also be considered a shot against the percentages. This disadvantage is negated to some degree for the righthander, since the average player hits with more control

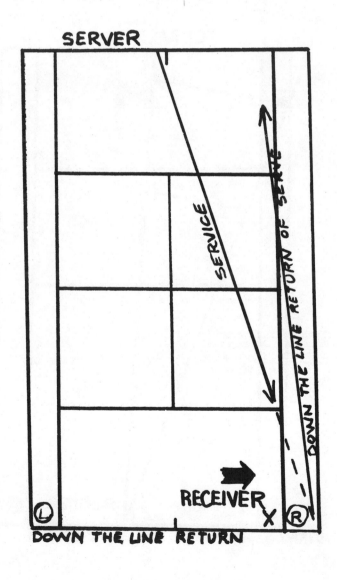

from the forehand. It is also noteworthy that the net is six inches higher at the posts, a fact that must be kept in mind when contemplating a shot of such precision. It is obvious that while this is a most desirable return, there is also a certain amount of risk involved. The server's reactions to a return of this type always vary, and depend directly on how far out of position he is pulled and how adept he is at compensating for a situation of this type. In any case, after drawing the server wide to the right, the most logical passing alternative is back to the opposite side, left. Like any sequence however, it should always be varied with shots back to the right side, as well as with lobs over the server's head.

Another alternative available to the receiver is crosscourt. A shot

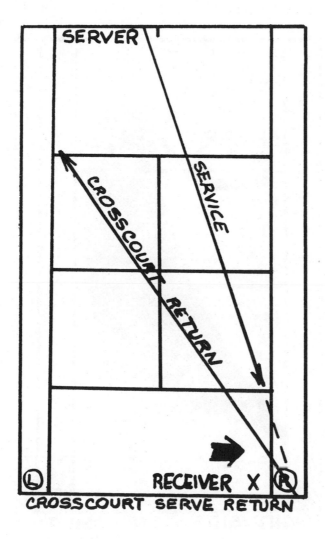

CROSSCOURT SERVE RETURN

of this type crosses the lowest part of the net, in the center, and travels along the diagonal of the court. The diagonal of any rectangle is, of course, its longest line. This added distance, plus the obvious fact that the ball crosses the entire width of the court, makes this a rather safe shot. While it must be considered a percentage shot in this respect, it nevertheless has the inherent disadvantage of crossing in front of the server rushing the net. However, this does not serve as a problem to the receiver that positions himself close to the baseline, returning the ball as soon after the bounce as possible. A return of this type will pass in front of the server before he has reached his volleying position. When he does volley it, he will do so from a position to the extreme left side of the court. Complete reversal of server initiative is attained by directing the passing shot to the area of vulnerability consequently created on the right.

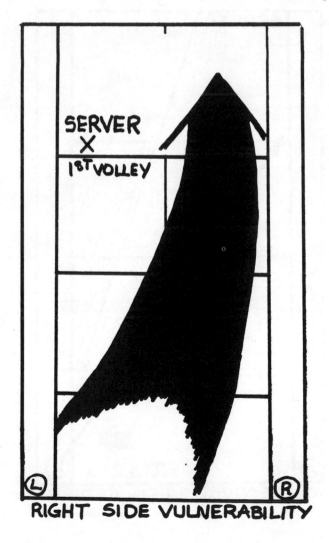

RIGHT SIDE VULNERABILITY

INSIDE-CORNER DEUCE COURT

The excessively fast Cannonball service is well suited for use to the inside corner of the deuce court. Its speed is multiplied since the distance from the server to the impact point of the ball is less. The negative side of this element of multiplied speed is that it cuts even shorter the time available to reach volleying position at the net. The effect of this serve is usually very good, however, since it must be returned by the righthander's backhand. The fact that the serve is being directed down the center of the court brings to mind the well-known "Center Theory" that speculates that any ball hit down the middle of the court has the desirable effect of forcing the opponent to create his own angle on his return. This line of thought is especially applicable here because of the difficulty most receivers expe-

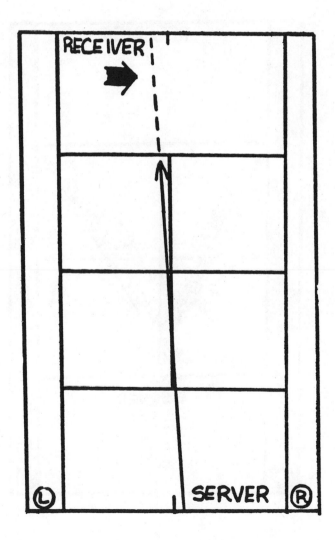

rience when attempting constructive placement of a serve of excessive speed from the backhand. The inability of the receiver to achieve consistent angled placement sends frequent service returns back down the middle also, thereby presenting the server with an identical situation on his first volley. The server must direct the ball with some constructive placement at this point, since the receiver is well positioned in the center of the court prepared to meet, or possibly reverse, the server initiative. In this circumstance, it is most desirable to volley the return of serve crosscourt and short, irrespective of whether it is taken as a forehand or backhand. A crosscourt shot of this type will do more immediate damage to the opponent than any. The down-the-line volley is less desirable because the ball stays over the playing area after the bounce, whereas the angled shot cross-

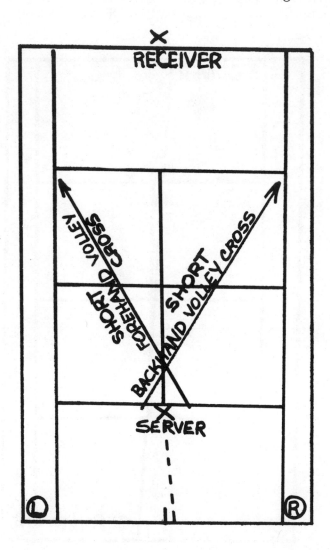

court often necessitates play from outside the playing area. By drawing the receiver inside the court, as well as to one side, he is maneuvered into a vulnerable position for a second and final volley deep and behind him to the opposite side. Again, it is desirable to shade to the side of the court that the first volley was hit, thus dissecting the potential angle of the opponent's return. If the return is high or defensive, an attempt to put the ball away and win the point outright should be made. This can be done effectively by volleying *deep*, either down the line or crosscourt. The depth of the shot is very important, since the well-placed ball close to the baseline limits significantly any play after the bounce.

Responses

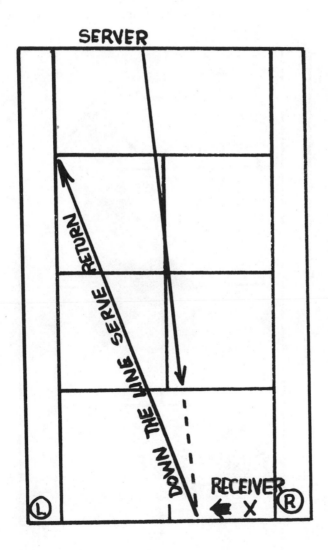

In order to reverse the initiative of the flat service to the inside corner of the deuce court, the receiver must overcome the lack of angle provided by the direction of the serve. Many times this is not an easy task because of the excessive speed that characterizes such a serve. It is not uncommon to return a serve hit this hard late. In this context, the wisest alternative would be down-the-line, since contacting the ball slightly late is a necessary element of the shot. The path of this ball is considered down-the-line, not because of its relation to any of the court stripes, but rather because it is contacted on the left side of the player executing it and stays on that side after it reaches its destination. Whether a shot is to be considered crosscourt or down-the-line is directly dependent on its relation to the man executing the shot. If it is contacted on his left and crosses to his right after the bounce, it is deemed crosscourt. If it remains on the same

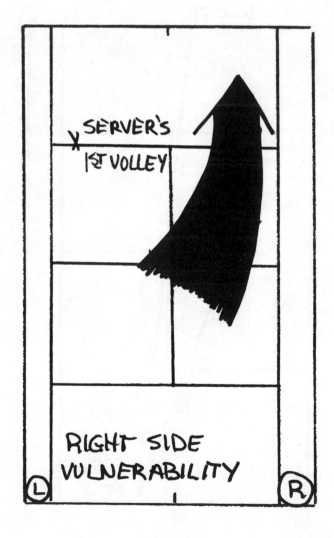

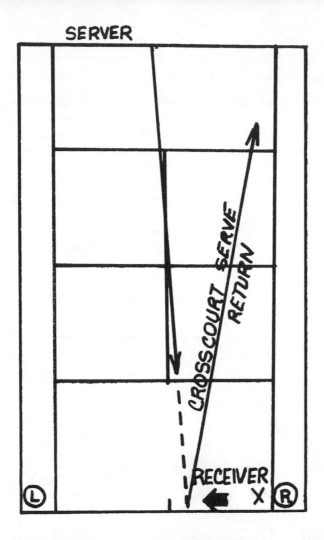

Returning serve from the inside corner leads the receiver toward a good defensive position in the center of the court, behind the baseline.

side that it was hit, it is considered down-the-line. When executed properly, a return of this type will pull the receiver wide left, thus opening an area of vulnerability on the right side. It is to this side that the majority of the receiver's passing shots should be directed. Whether this final passing shot is executed through the use of the forehand or backhand is directly dependent on the direction of the server's response to the service return. These responses will, of course, always vary with the individual server's abilities and his estimation of how to cope with the event at hand.

The second alternative available to the receiver is crosscourt. This is a difficult return off of a service of this type since the excessive pace on the ball must be completely overcome in order to contact the ball early, thereby directing it crosscourt. The players that make

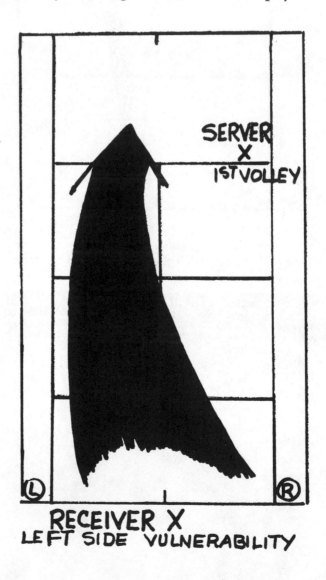

RECEIVER X
LEFT SIDE VULNERABILITY

this shot with any consistency at all have exceptional quickness and capacity for anticipation. There are degrees of success to this return, as with any, with the ones closest to the sideline, of course, being the most successful. If the shot is, indeed, crosscourt, it will force the server and elicit a defensive or mediocre volley the majority of the time. When this happens, the receiver is in an excellent position to complete the initiative reversal, since receiving from either of the inside corners necessarily leads one back to good defensive position in the center. The most obvious conclusion to the sequence is a passing shot to the left side of the court. Like any sequence, however, it should be varied and mixed with other passing alternatives back to the right, behind the server who anticipated the shot but committed himself too early, or with lobs over his head.

INSIDE-CORNER ADD COURT

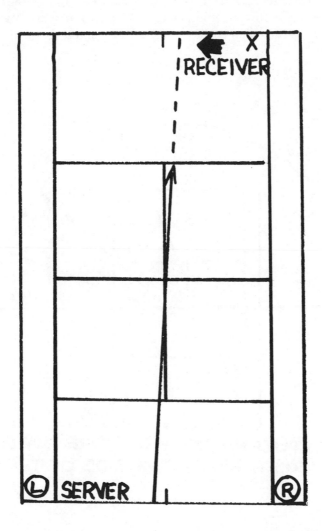

The inside corners are well suited for use of the Cannonball service. The distance from the server to the impact point of the ball in the service court is less than either diagonal track to the outside corners. This is complemented by the fact that the net is six inches lower in the center. These two factors serve to multiply both the speed and probability of success for the server in this corner. It is worth noting, however, that just as pace of the ball is increased, so is the time available to the server to reach good volleying position *decreased*. In correspondence with the "Center Theory," many returns from this service will be directed back down the middle of the court. This theory in effect states that it is possible to use a ball hit down the center constructively, since it forces the receiver to create his own angle on his return. It is much easier to hit an angled placement from a position to one side of the court, rather than the center. The fact that it is received from near the center of the court has a negative effect as well, since any serve to this corner naturally leads the receiver toward good defensive position when preparing to receive the server's first volley. With this in mind, it is imperative

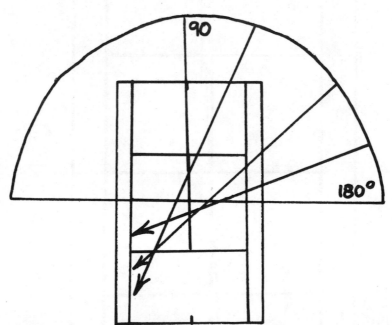

ANGLED PLACEMENTS ARE MORE NATURAL
FROM POSITIONS TO THE SIDE OF THE COURT

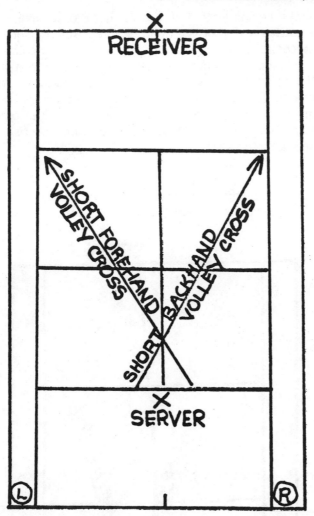

that this first volley be executed constructively, in a manner that will do the most to dislodge the receiver from a position of such security. This is accomplished most effectively with a volley short and crosscourt, irrespective of whether it is encountered on the forehand or backhand side. A shot of this type moves the opponent away from the center of the court, by forcing him to cope with the crosscourt angle, and inside it in his effort to compensate for its lack of depth. When executed properly, the receiver often finds himself in a very precarious position not only to the side of the court, but inside it as well. A position such as this leaves an obvious area of vulnerability to the opposite side of the court, behind him. While this is an ideal response to the low or aggressive return of serve, an attempt should always be made to put the high or defensive return away. It is essential that a shot of this type be deep, since a shot close to the baseline necessarily limits much of the play possible after the bounce. I recommend dominant usage of crosscourt placement because of the angle away from the court that it naturally creates. This angle draws the opponent away from the center of the court and puts him in a position where use of the down-the-line placement can be used effectively without much of the inherent risk that otherwise accompanies the shot.

Responses

When receiving the flat serve from the inside corner, the receiver has the relative advantage of being able to return the ball

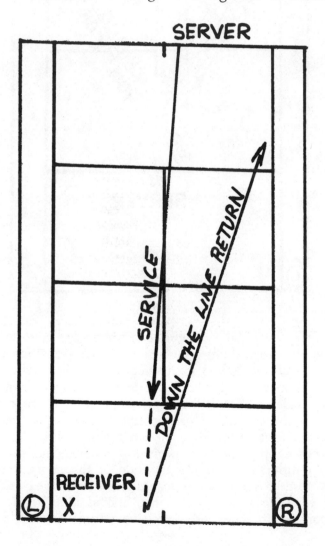

with his forehand. Speed is without a doubt the dominant characteristic of the Cannonball service, and it will be forcing no matter
which side it is received by. The high-speed factor often elicits returns contacted late, thus making a return down-the-line very
natural, since hitting the ball slightly late is an essential part of its
execution. Such a shot closely resembles the return of serve necessary
in doubles to keep the ball away from the opposing netman.
If caught soon after the bounce and hit with enough angle, it is a
shot that will draw the server wide to the right, thus beginning the
sequence of initiative reversal. The sequence is logically followed with
the succeeding shot directed to the area of vulnerability created wide to the left. While the majority of the receiver's passing

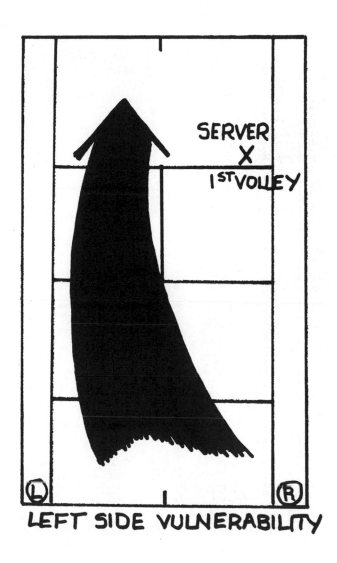

LEFT SIDE VULNERABILITY

shots are best directed to this area of the court, it is wise to vary the sequence patterns with shots back to the right or with lobs over the server crowding the net too close.

Another, but more difficult, return of serve is crosscourt. It must be considered more difficult since the excessive pace of the serve must be fully compensated for in order to contact the ball early enough to attain such a placement. A return of this type is easier said than done, since the speed of the serve is at a maximum because of the reduced distance necessary for the ball to travel to any inside corner. Though this response is the most difficult, it is also the most decisive. The ball never passes in front of the server and will, because of its early hit, reduce even more the time available to the server in his rush to the net. Server reaction to this shot is very

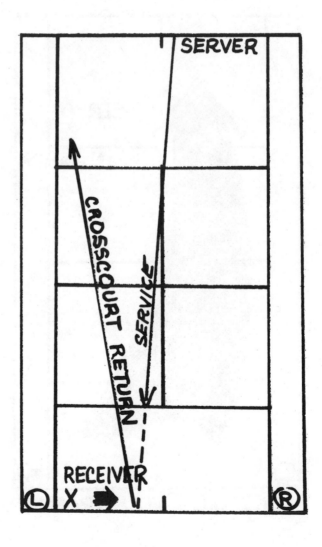

SERVER
X
1ST VOLLEY

RIGHT SIDE VULNERABILITY

often defensive, a fact that sets the stage for complete initiative reversal by the receiver. This return pulls the server wide to the left, thus leaving an area of vulnerability wide to the right side. It is to this side of the court that the majority of the receiver's passing shots are best directed, while at the same time remaining aware of the negative effect that often occurs from the establishment of patterns too rigid and without variety. On the higher levels of play, anticipation of this type often spells the difference between winning and losing.

OUTSIDE-CORNER ADD COURT

The outside corner of the add court lends itself well to the use

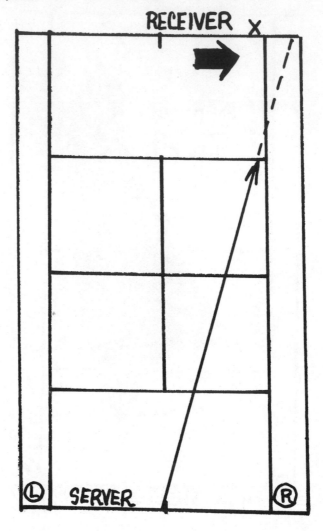

of the Cannonball serve. This very fast serve must be received by the righthanded player's backhand, and travels the longer diagonal path across the court, a fact that leaves the server considerably more margin for error. The serve does cross a higher portion of the net, near the posts, and this fact must be recognized and reflected in the successful server's delivery. The diagonal flight of the ball negates any advantage formerly gained from the inside corner, with respect to its minimum distance from the server to impact point within the court and its secondary effect of multiplying the given speed of the serve as a result of its traveling a lesser distance. Serves to the outside corners do, however, create a desirable angle that leads the receiver off the playing area and into a vulnerable position for the next shot. This fact lends itself particularly well to the server rushing the net, since such a pattern limits even more the time available for the receiver to recover and reach good defensive position back in the center of the court, behind the baseline. If the return of serve is low or unusually well placed, it is wise to place the first volley short on the left side of the court. This is obviously executed by means of a backhand volley down-the-line or a forehand volley crosscourt. In any instance where the opponent is pulled wide of the court, the wisest play is to the opening on the opposite side, irrespective of whether this must be accomplished through the use of a forehand or backhand. This strategy is diametrically opposed to that prescribed for response to shots, serves or otherwise, that are

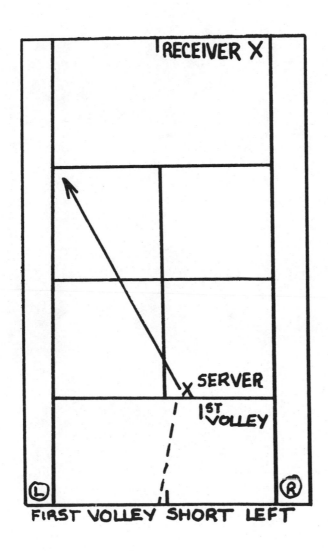

FIRST VOLLEY SHORT LEFT

Touch volley crosscourt.

directed down-the-middle, the wisest strategy of which employs the use of the angled shot crosscourt. In essence then, serves to the outside corners are best handled by placements with reference to the opponent and his position on the court, while service returns from the inside corners are most wisely executed by placement with reference to the player executing the shot. Whether a shot is deemed crosscourt or down-the-line is, of course, always judged with reference to whether the shot in question passes from one side of the man hitting the ball to the other. The down-the-line ball stays on the same side of the player that it was hit, while the crosscourt passes from one side to the other. Neither have any reference to the lines on the court or whether it crosses from one side to the other. Thus, the wisest response to a return off of a serve to the outside add corner, is to the left side of the court, deep to the corner when the return is weak or defensive, and short, near the intersection of the service and side lines, when it is low or well placed. The short ball pulls the receiver inside the court, as well as to one side, thereby setting the stage for a final volley by the server deep to the right. It is always wise to employ the use of the potential percentage angle concept discussed earlier, and this is no exception. Shading to the side of the court the opponent is hitting from is a universal application and an essential element of the anticipation necessary to play successfully in top-flight tennis today.

Responses

Returning the Cannonball serve from the outside add corner is often difficult since the ball travels very fast to the backhand and increases in angle as it progresses. Because of this, it is not practical to stand extremely far behind the baseline in an effort to compensate for its excessive speed since it is very unlikely that a receiver would possess enough speed afoot to compensate for the increasing angle of the serve. It is best to return the serve from as near the baseline as possible. The inherent speed of the Cannonball serve often elicits a return hit late, and the down-the-line return uses this fact to best advantage since contacting the ball slightly late is an essential element of the shot. It cannot be considered a percentage shot because of relatively small area of the court necessary to hit between the server's reach and the sideline. It is a very controlled shot since much of its flight is often outside the playing area as well as over the highest portion of the net near the posts. The nature of its placement makes a very aggressive shot, many times not only sufficient to begin a sequence of initiative reversal, but to win the point outright as well. The down-the-line return is one that draws the server wide to the left side of the court, thus providing an opening for the receiver's final passing shot to the right. It is essential

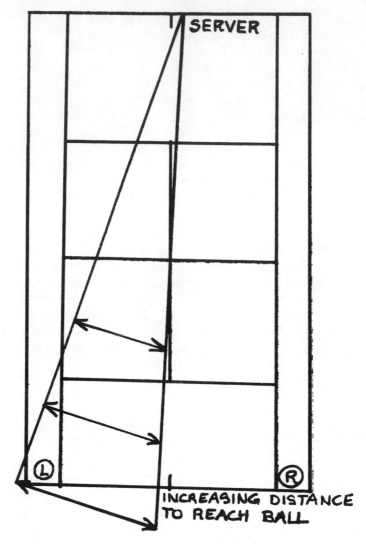

that the receiver return quickly to the center of the baseline, since his right side is open as well, should the server volley his return crosscourt.

An alternate response to the down-the-line return is crosscourt. The flight of the crosscourt is advantageous and with the percentages since, in this case, the ball travels across the width of the court and over the lowest portion of the net in the center. Unfortunately, however, the difficulty of this shot arises from its physical execution, and not from any particular liability with respect to its flight or relation to the court. The Cannonball service is hit extremely hard, as its name correctly implies, and it is often difficult to compensate suffi-

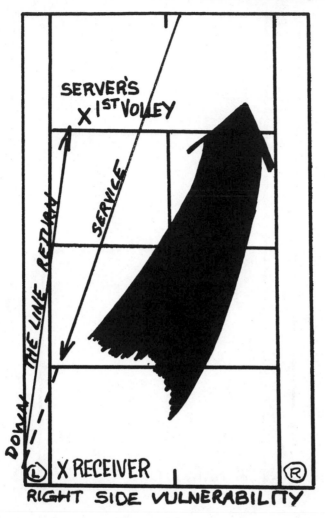

ciently for its rapidly increasing angle, necessary to enable the receiver to contact the ball early enough to direct it crosscourt. The difficulty factor of this return is further complicated by the fact that it must be returned via the right-handed player's backhand, the weaker side for many. In essence, the receiver is faced with having to return one of the server's most aggressive initiatives from a position wide of the court, with his often weaker backhand side. When the shot is executed successfully, its effect is desirable, necessarily pulling the server wide to the right side of the court for his first volley. This act immediately creates an area of vulnerability on the left side of the court, and it is to this area that the majority of the receiver's final passing shots should be directed. It is extremely important that the receiver recover quickly from his position wide left after

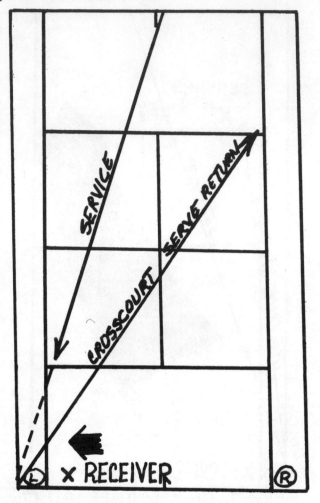

making the initial service return since the right side of his court is open, as well, for exploitation by the server. Successful initiative reversal in this sequence is dependent on both a forcing return and quick recovery into good position to play the server's first volley aggressively.

There are many theories of strategy and tactics that remain the same in subsequent chapters. However, the effects of differing service spins are profound and very individual, as they begin each sequence. It is in this light that the next chapters deal with the Slice, Topspin, and American Twist respectively.

LEFT SIDE VULNERABILITY

8

THE SLICE SERVICE

OUTSIDE-CORNER DEUCE COURT

Slice services vary in speed and spin, with each predominant characteristic having its own peculiar assets and liabilities with respect to

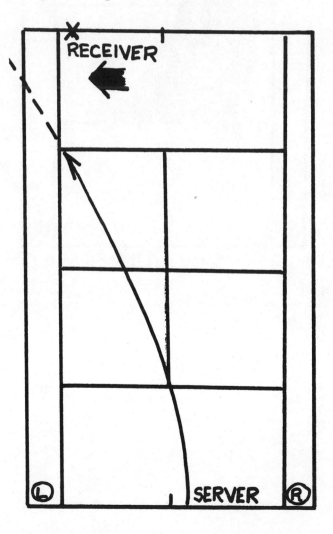

their effect on individual players. The hard Slice is characterized by its speed, with the spin acting as a secondary agent for control, while the full Slice is characterized by an extreme excess of side spin left.

The outside corner of the deuce court is more natural than any for the right-handed player serving the Slice since the natural serving motion is right to left and the outside corner of the deuce court is to the left of the server's position on the baseline. The hard and full Slice are both well suited for use to this corner, with the excess spin left of the full Slice pulling most radically away from the receiver. The fact that this serve does lead the receiver away from the playing area inevitably opens the right side of the court for exploitation by the wise server. It is again to the server's advantage to employ the use of the potential percentage angle concept, this time

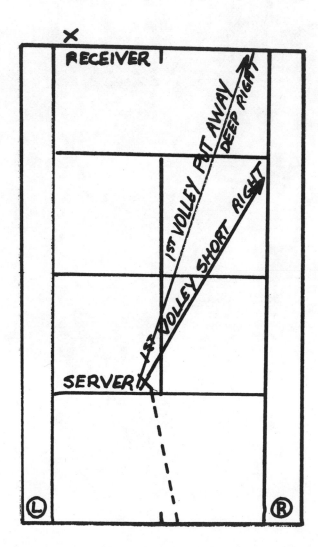

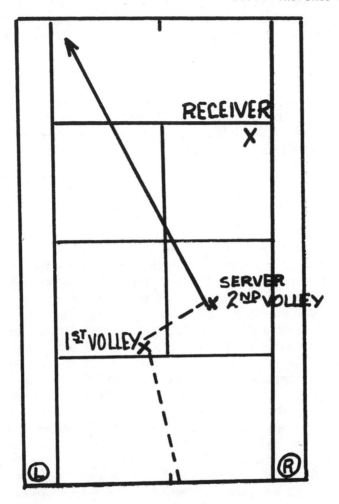

shading to the left side of the center line as he rushes the net for proper position to execute the first volley. This first volley is most effectively placed to the opening on the right side of the court, short and approximately at the intersection of the service and side lines. This is the first volley and, while it may be put away at times, it should be thought of as a preparation for a second and final volley. However, if the return of serve is defensive and above the level of the net, the first volley should similarly be directed to the right side, but deep rather than short, with the intention of winning the point outright. A shot of this type deep to the corner is more decisive than the shot of short angle, since it substantially limits the possibility of play after the bounce. When not attempting to conclude the point with the first volley, one should move closer to the net and slightly to the right of the center line for the second volley. Such a move again dissects the potential angle of the receiver's return. The succeeding volley from this position is most logically directed deep to the left side of the court, behind the opponent successfully drawn inside the playing area by the first volley. In order to avoid undue anticipation, one should be very reluctant of establishing patterns too constant. With this in mind, it is often wise to alternate the primary sequence back to the left, behind the man committing himself too early, and with lobs over his head.

Responses

The favorable response to the Slice service depends to a large extent on one's ability to anticipate its execution before it is hit. Use of the Eastern backhand or Continental grip and a service toss to the right are the basic ingredients necessary to attain the curve left of the Slice, and while it is impossible to see an opponent's grip changes, one can observe the position of the server's toss. Careful observation here can often give the receiver that split second of anticipation necessary to make an effective return of serve.

The return from which one has the greatest percentage of success is short and crosscourt. It is correctly deemed the percentage alternative since the net is six inches lower in the center, the area over which this return travels. It allows for a maximum margin for error by crossing the width of the court during its flight. When defensive or ineffective, however, the crosscourt return has the notable disadvantage of crossing and hanging in front of the server, thus allowing for easy access and probable aggressive play. When kept low and directed with adequate angle, it can be very effective, and it is in this light that it will be treated. When executed in this manner, it can reverse the initiative that originated with the server by forcing him to volley defensively from below the level of the net. It is at this point in the sequence that the receiver should make his most aggressive attempt to seize the initiative. After such a move, the most obvious opening is to the opposite side of the court, to the right. While passing shots are most effective with the dipping action of topspin, there can be no absolute concerning either the technique used or their direction. Both will vary with respect to the individual strengths and weaknesses of the receiver hitting the shot, as well as his estimation of the opponent's general vulnerability at the time. In any event, the choices should not be made at intervals too regular, in order to eliminate any chance of the undue anticipation that often detracts from an otherwise good shot.

Another excellent return, but one of higher risk, is down-the-line. When drawn off the court by the excess spin of the Slice, the flight of a return of this type will often pass over an area outside of

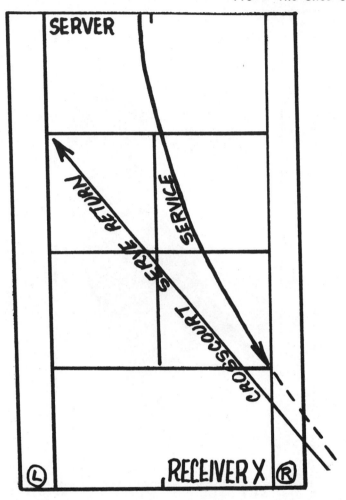

the playing surface. This obviously leaves substantially less margin for error than the crosscourt return, the flight of which passes over the entire court surface. The down-the-line response to the Slice service, in this court, is a touch shot where feel for a ball sliding away is a necessity. The fact that the net is higher near the posts, as well as the relatively small area of the court necessary to hit, both contribute to the inherent difficulty of a shot that must be considered against the percentages. It is most wisely used when ahead, and in a position in the match where it is possible to afford such a chance. As a change of pace, it is well used as a subtle, but very firm, reminder to the opponent that the down-the-line alternative is at your disposal, and a shot to be guarded against. When executed successfully, it will draw the server wide to the right side of the court, thereby

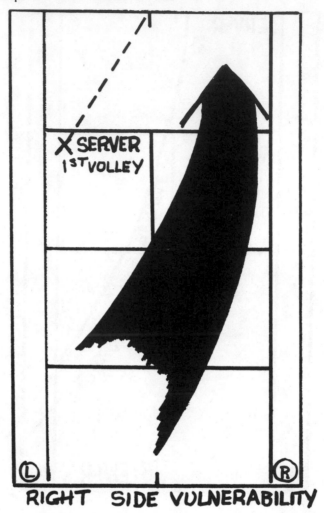

RIGHT SIDE VULNERABILITY

creating an area of vulnerability to the left. A defensive volley is particularly likely from this return since it forces the opponent on his backhand side. It is noteworthy, however, that with all of the advantages just mentioned, the receiver leaves himself in a very precarious position should it be returned crosscourt to his backhand side. The down-the-line return takes less time to reach its destination than the crosscourt, thus making a volley crosscourt by the server very difficult to reach since the receiver has just returned serve from a position wide to the right side of the court.

It is not always possible to anticipate an upcoming serve, and every player is caught off guard at times. It is under these circumstances that the intermediate level player often makes a very fun-

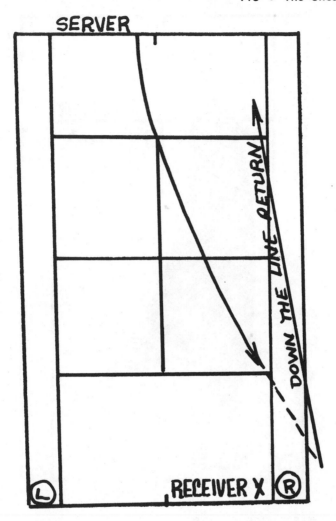

SERVER

DOWN THE LINE RETURN

L

RECEIVER X R

damental error, that being the lunging hundred-mile-per-hour put-away attempt. The most realistic alternative in any instance such as this, is, ironically, the lob—a shot that can provide enough time for the player to recover and get back into good defensive position. When receiving the unexpected or overwhelming serve, such a shot is a much wiser alternative than either the one hundred-to-one stab or the floating return back down the middle into the waiting hands of an eager netman.

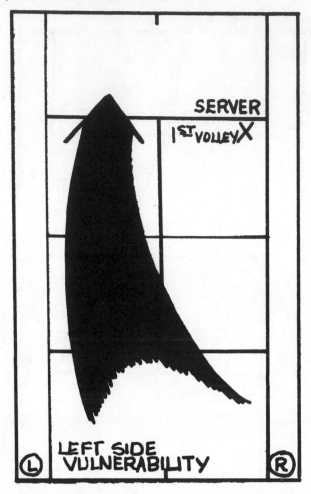

SERVER

1ST VOLLEY X

LEFT SIDE VULNERABILITY

L   R

INSIDE-CORNER DEUCE COURT

The Slice service makes different use of its natural spin when served to the inside corner of the deuce court, since curve left directs the ball toward the receiver rather than away as was the case with the outside corner. The excess curve of the full Slice induces the ball to bounce INTO the receiver, causing most receivers to crowd their return. A cramped swing inhibits any return, often causing a weak or defensive response. The hard Slice can also be effectively used to this corner as a forcing shot to the righthanded opponent's backhand. This corner is conducive to the use of serves of great speed, where their angle into the court is more direct, since the net is six inches lower in the center and the total distance from the server to the impact point of the ball in the court less.

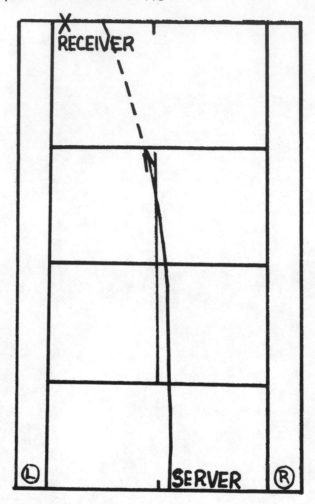

Many players choose to use the Slice service over the completely flat Cannonball since the spin offers an additional degree of control with relatively little sacrifice in speed. This serve does not pull the opponent off the court, as was the case with the Slice to the outside corner, but rather leads him back toward the center. According to the well-known "Center Theory," any time a player hits from a position in the center of the court, he is forced to create his own angle on his return. In other words, it is much easier to hit angled returns when one is off to one side of the court, rather than squarely in the middle, as is the case with this serve. This is advantageous to the server as long as he acknowledges the fact that he must overcome the same circumstances when presented with a majority of returns back down the middle, as well. This response pattern is particularly likely to

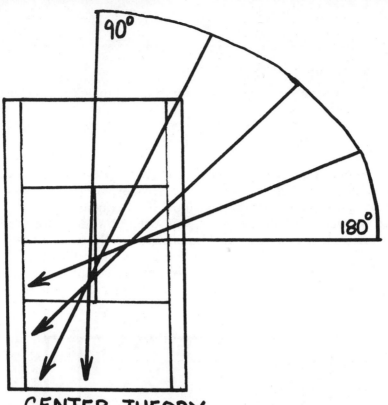

90°

180°

CENTER THEORY

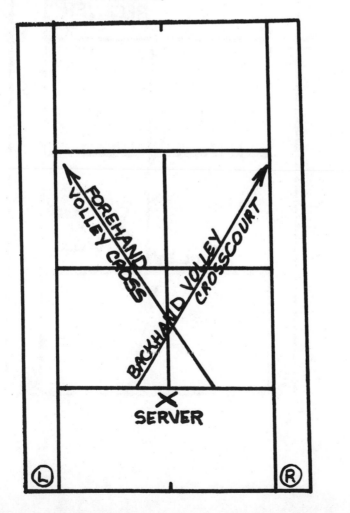

FOREHAND VOLLEY CROSS

BACKHAND VOLLEY CROSSCOURT

X
SERVER

Ⓛ　　　Ⓡ

occur, since it is being returned by the righthander's backhand, a side from which many players experience a lesser degree of control. With the server's first volley being one of such importance, it is again wise to employ the use of the short shot crosscourt, since it readily pulls the opponent inside the court, as well as to one side. This strategy immediately puts the receiving player in an awkward position to receive the server's second volley, directed deep to the opposite side of the court behind him. This sequence, as any, should never become constant, since patterns without variety are easily anticipated, a fact that can contribute significantly to eventual player downfall. If his response to either the full or hard Slice is defensive or substantially above the level of the net, an attempt should be made to put the ball away and win the point outright. In an effort such

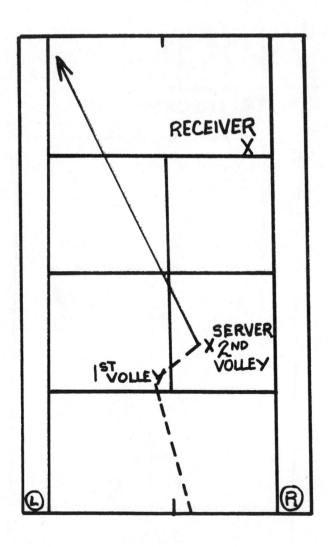

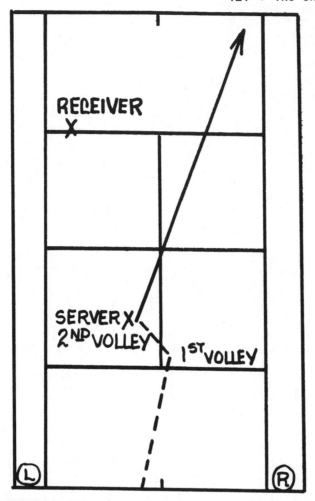

as this, the player seeks the most decisive shot at his disposal. While the crosscourt shot leads the opponent off of the playing area, no absolute can be established as far as any direction best suited for the put-away sequence. It is notable, however, that the depth of the shot plays a significant role in the ultimate success or failure of the attempt. A shot of this type should always be directed deep in the court, since added depth limits substantially any play after the bounce.

Responses

The most effective return of serve to the Slice service, directed to the inside corner of the deuce court, is crosscourt. Unfortunately, there are several notable obstacles to the execution of this shot that make it difficult and against the percentages. The righthanded receiver is faced not only with the prospect of returning the ball with his backhand but with having to hit the ball decidedly in front to a very small area of the court. This is a task of sizable proportions when one recalls the effect of the Slice to this corner, and its tendency to curve INTO the receiver. It is very difficult to contact a ball of this type early enough to redirect it crosscourt. It will often crowd the receiver, thus making it likely that a late return will result. The player making this shot must have a more than adequate backhand, as well as a thorough knowledge of the effects of the Slice in this corner, in order to fully compensate for their effects and implement the strategy crosscourt. When done properly, it is a very aggressive shot that is very likely to provide the punch necessary to instigate

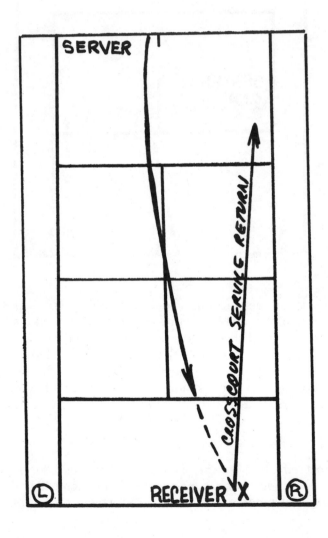

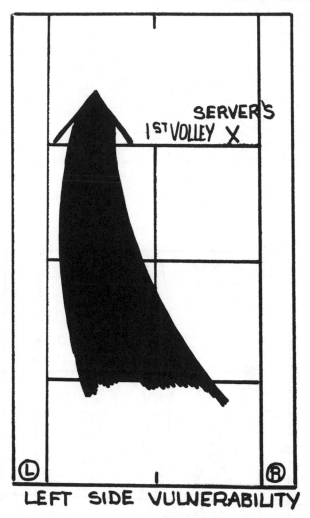

LEFT SIDE VULNERABILITY

the beginning of initiative reversal. It pulls the server wide to the right side of the court, thus creating an area of vulnerability to the left. It is to this side of the court that the majority of the receiver's passing shots should be directed. The means the receiver uses to achieve these ends will always vary, of course, and depend directly on the server's reaction to the wide volley to the right.

The fact that many returns to the Slice in this corner are contacted late make the down-the-line return the most consistently effective response at the receiver's disposal. It is very difficult to overcome either of the Slice serve alternatives (hard or full) to this corner since the tendency in both cases, is to contact the ball late. It has been pointed out in previous discussions that contacting the ball slightly late is an essential element of the down-the-line and it is readily apparent how such a shot would lend itself to these circumstances. It is a shot that closely parallels the return of serve necessary in doubles, when keeping the ball away from the opposing netman is a primary objective. The best response, in this instance, is short, hopefully catching the server before he is prepared to volley. If he is caught in "no-man's land," or pulled extremely wide of the court, a defensive volley will often result, thus leaving an area of vulnerability on the right side of the court. The concluding shot of the sequence should most often be directed to this side of the court, while wisely interspersing aspects of variety into the sequence, in order to avoid the development of unnecessary anticipation.

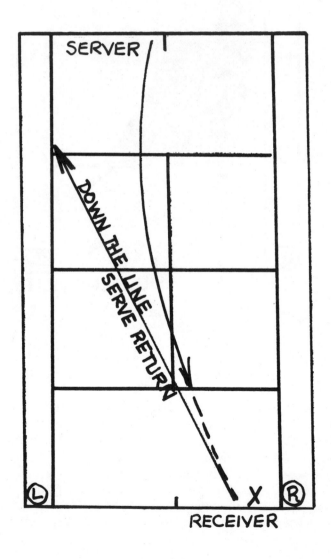

SERVER'S
X1 ST VOLLEY

RIGHT SIDE
VULNERABILITY

In any circumstances encountered on the tennis court, the player should always react with some positive intent. The wise player is not content to react one shot at a time, as the play develops. When on the receiving end of an extremely aggressive shot by the opponent, one should always retain that element of constructive play. When it is not possible to respond to the serve with a directional placement, a conscious attempt should, nevertheless, be made to keep the ball low. The effects of the "Center Theory" are relevant in all cases, thus making the low return, even though down the center, a direct challenge to the retainment of server initiative. The successful tennis player is a thinking man, where the mental exchange of attack and defense is a constant challenge—an outlook that supersedes the comparatively shallow pastime of aimlessly knocking the ball across the net without constructive intent.

INSIDE-CORNER ADD COURT

When used to the inside corner of the add court, the Slice service contains characteristics discussed with respect to both corners of the deuce court. The fact that it is directed to an inside corner allows the server to reap the rewards of the net being lower in the center, with the additional fact of the distance from the server to impact point in the court being less also acting to his advantage. Both of these characteristics serve to complement and indirectly increase the speed of the service. The lower level of the net obviously allows for a much safer margin for error, while the lesser distance between the server and his aiming point reduces the time necessary for the ball, traveling at a given speed, to reach its destination. The "full"

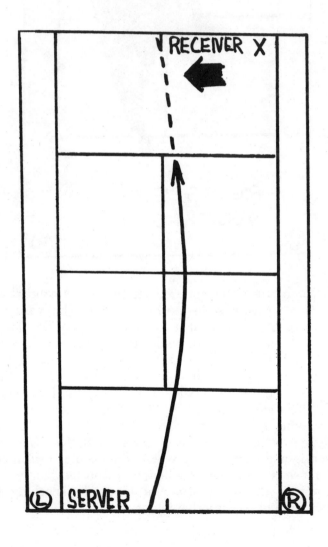

and "hard" Slice services are both applicable for successful use in this corner, when interspersed with other serves of differing speeds, spins, and direction. The ball served to this corner has the relative disadvantage of always being received by the righthanded player's forehand and leading him back toward good defensive position in the center of the court. Play from the center of the court again brings to mind the inevitable implications of the "Center Theory," which in effect states that the player hitting from the center of the court is forced to create his own angle on his return. This is a very relevant theory, with its use being recently exemplified by many women in their efforts to overcome the pinpoint placement and consistency of the young American Chris Evert's groundstrokes. Her flawless play from the baseline is only multiplied when she is given the oppor-

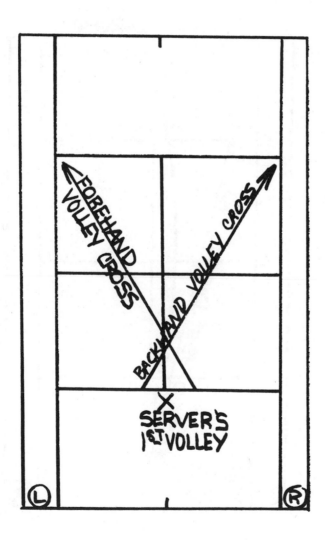

tunity to hit from the side of the court, where her angle is the greatest. The Slice service to the inside corner of the add court negates an advantage of this type, many times serving to induce a return of serve back down the middle, as well, thus forcing the server to overcome the same circumstance on his first volley. This is most readily done by directing the first volley short and crosscourt, irrespective of whether it is encountered as a forehand or backhand. A shot of this type draws the receiver inside the playing area, as well as to one side. This is a fundamental aggressive sequence, since it immediately creates an area of vulnerability deep to the opposite side, behind him. If the initial return of serve is weak or defensive, an attempt to put the ball away outright should be made. The put-

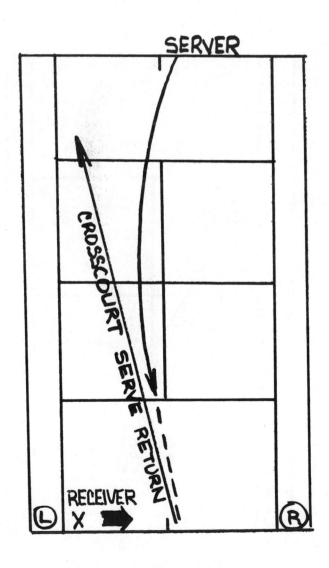

away sequence is most decisive when directed deep to either side of the court, since it substantially limits any play after the bounce.

Responses

The most aggressive response to the Slice service to the inside corner of the add court, is crosscourt. It is a relatively difficult shot to execute, but with the difficulty being somewhat lessened by the fact that it is being received by the righthanded player's forehand. Because the ball is being directed crosscourt, which in essence means across the body of the man executing the shot from his right to left side in this case, the ball must be contacted early. There is less margin for error, in this shot than others, since the ball must be placed within the relatively small area of the court, between the server rushing the net and the sideline. The ball will cross the net over

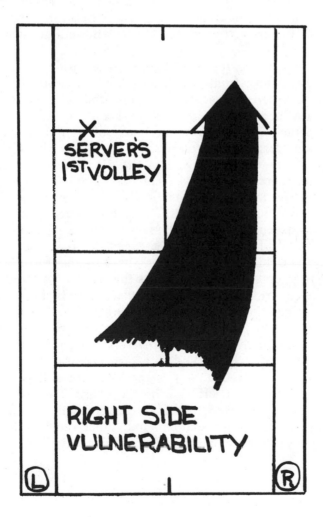

its higher portions near the posts, a fact that contributes, additionally, to the difficulty of the shot. This is very often the response to a slower second serve, where the spin is not in excess, and adjustment to it not a dominant factor. The strength of the sequence is reinforced by the fact that, by being received from an inside corner, the receiver is led back to good defensive position in the center of the court. The return itself will pull the server wide to the left in his attempt to execute his first volley, a fact that leaves a decided area of vulnerability on the opposite side of the court to the right. It is to this opening that the majority of the receiver's passing shots should be directed. The fact that the receiver occupies such an enviable position in the center of the court makes him readily accessible to most any response by the server. It is in this context that the server finds himself at the relative mercy of the receiver who, while directing the majority of his passing shots to the obvious opening on the right, should consciously inject a variety of placements and change-ups, in order to prevent the establishment of patterns too regular.

The down-the-line response to the Slice inside is also very useful, being the return from which most players center their receiving attack. It is a percentage shot and one that closely resembles the service return necessary in doubles to keep the ball away from the opposing netman. It is considered more of a percentage shot than the crosscourt from this corner, since it crosses the lowest portion of the net, in the center, as well as the diagonal of the court, a fact that increases considerably the receiver's margin for error. When executed properly, it is a shot that leads the server wide to the right, very often eliciting a defensive response, since the server's volley must be executed via his backhand, from a position many times below the level of the net. This is especially the case when the receiver positions himself on or near the baseline for his return. An attacking position such as this allows the receiver to contact the ball earlier, thereby rushing the server even more in his charge to the net since, as mentioned earlier, the natural speed factor of any serve is multiplied when used to the inside corners, because the distance from the server to the impact in the service court is less. When executed properly, the down-the-line return necessarily pulls the server wide to the right, a fact that sets the stage for a final passing shot, by the receiver, to the left side of the court. The exact means by which the ball is directed to this destination will, of course, always vary according to server reaction, individual receiver assessment of the situation at hand, and his decision on how to best cope with it.

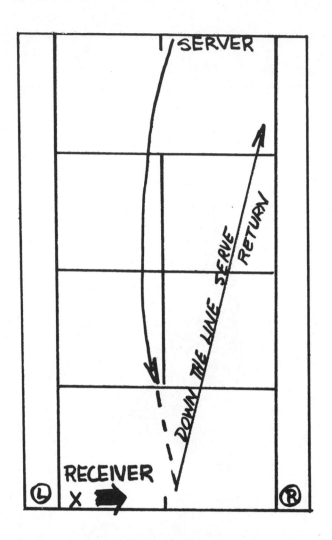

An aggressive down-the-line service return.

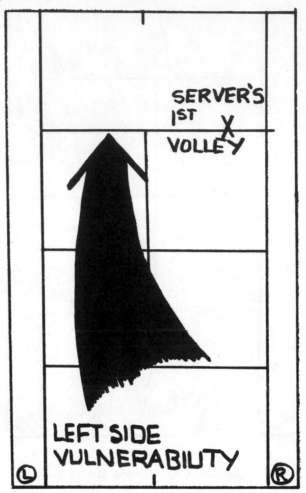

OUTSIDE-CORNER ADD COURT

It is difficult to use the natural spin of the full Slice in the out-side corner of this court, since one is serving from a position to the left of the corner at which one is aiming a "side left" serve. When the righthanded server serves a Slice in the deuce court, his physical position is still to the right of the service court to which he is aiming. He is able, therefore, to work from the natural arc of the curve left Slice. This left curve of the Slice is most radical in the outside corner of the deuce court and becomes less so as one moves to the right toward the outside add corner. It is for this reason that the outside corner of the add court is the most unnatural for the right-handed server. Close observation has shown that many righthanders

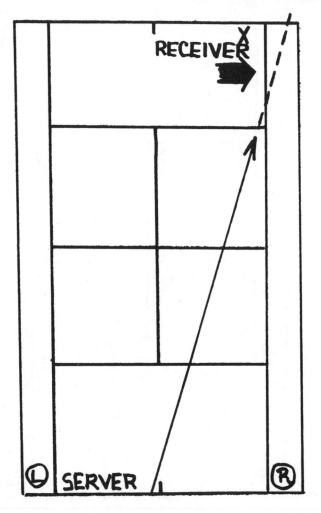

hit this corner through some kind of compensation, either with their toss over their head to the left, thereby creating more of an angle to the corner, or with their body position with relation to the baseline. The most natural serve to this corner for the right hander is the American Twist, since the toss is necessarily over the server's head, thereby setting the stage for spin left to right, as opposed to right to left when serving the Slice. A hard Slice is effective in this corner due to its speed, because it is received by any righthander's backhand, and because it leads the receiver off the court as he retrieves it. If the serve was exceptionally hard, well placed, or to an unusually weak backhand, the service return will often be weak. Such a return will come from a wide angle outside of the court and will many times be late, consequently calling for a shade right by

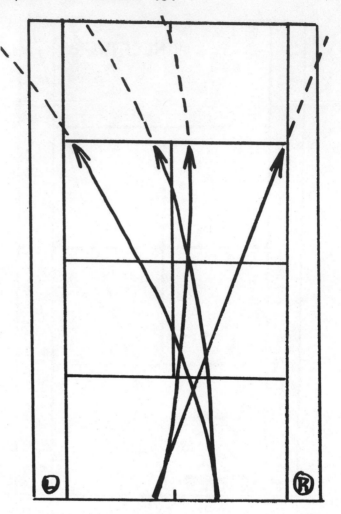

Curve left becomes less radical as one moves from the outside deuce corner to the outside add.

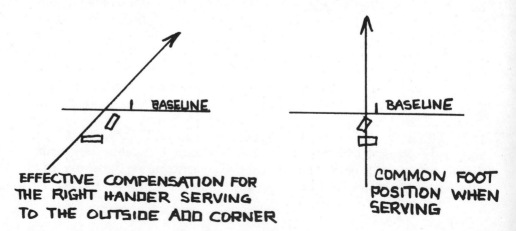

EFFECTIVE COMPENSATION FOR
THE RIGHT HANDER SERVING
TO THE OUTSIDE ADD CORNER

COMMON FOOT
POSITION WHEN
SERVING

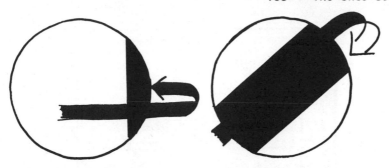

THE SLICE SERVICE —
THE BALL IS CONTACTED ON ITS
RIGHT SIDE, THUS IMPARTING A
SIDE SPIN FROM RIGHT TO LEFT

THE AMERICAN TWIST —
THE BALL IS BRUSHED ON
ITS BACK SIDE DIAGONALLY
FROM LEFT TO RIGHT

the net rusher in order to dissect the ever-changing percentage angle of the opponent's return. Having pulled the opponent off the court to the right, the net rusher's first volley should most often be placed short to the left side of the court. The short first volley, as a response to a low or aggressive return of serve, not only brings the opponent across the court, but draws him inside it as well, a position that immediately makes him vulnerable for a second and final volley behind him back to the right. These are primary patterns but should not be considered absolutes. The wise player will vary these patterns with secondary volleys of differing depths and speeds as well as with volleys back to the right side behind the opponent, anticipating the shot but committing himself too early. This element of variety can serve as a deterrent to the anticipation that is often the undoing of an otherwise good shot. If the response to the service was defensive, the first volley should be put away, with the thought of ending the point outright. It is possible for this to be done with a short-angled volley, but decisive results are more often found by hitting deep to the left corner, since the initial service has pulled the receiver wide right in order to make his return.

It should be noted at this point that in all of the volley sequence patterns discussed thus far, as well as those to follow, thorough knowledge of the potential percentage angle concept was essential. All diagrams indicate shading left or right when anticipating the return of an opponent hitting from a position of angle, off or at one side of the playing area. J. Parmly Paret states this thought well in his *Psychology and Advanced Play* when he writes, "If the ball has been driven off to one side of the adversary's court, the playing center is far from the physical center. It is really the center of the angle be-

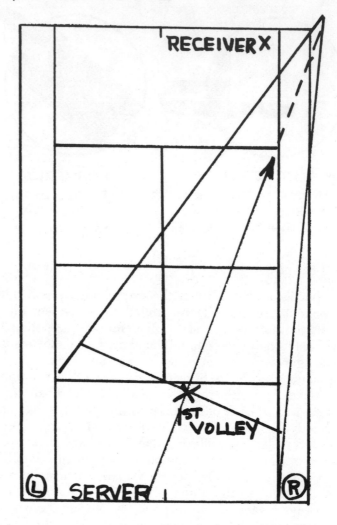

tween all possible lines of direction the ball can travel and still stay within the court."[1] A thorough familiarity with this principle is at the center of the professional's ability to play the exceptionally fast and aggressive games witnessed today. No amount of natural speed afoot is sufficient to compensate for practical applications of this axiom of advanced play.

1. J. Parmley Peret, *Psychology and Advanced Play*, Vol. III. The Lawn Tennis Library American Lawn Tennis Inc. New York: 1927, p. 94.

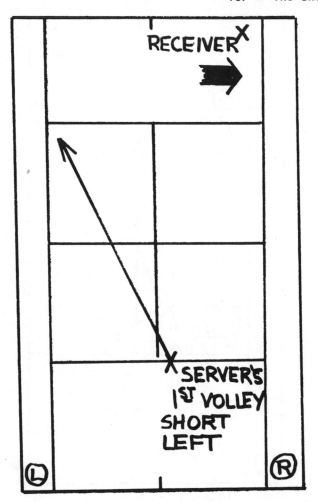

Responses

The Slice service to the outside corner of the add court will be received by the righthanded player's backhand, will lead the receiver off the court when retrieving it, and under most circumstances, will be a serve without an excess of spin left. The receiver will most often encounter a hard Slice (as opposed to the heavily spin-laden full Slice) usually on the first serve, or a slower delivery on the second serve where adjustment to the spin is not a dominant factor. One will rarely face the more difficult-to-manage full Slice in this corner, except when served by the lefthander whose natural corners are the reverse of the player who is righthanded.

A service to either outside corner leads the opponent off the court. If the service is effective, and draws a defensive return, the

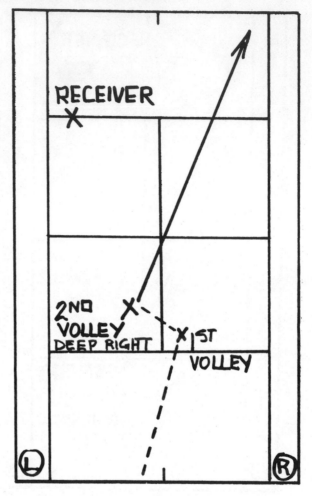

net rushing server is in a most favorable position for his first volley to the opposite side of the court. While this is an ideal initiative-response pattern, it is also one that is difficult to attain when, for one reason or another, the initiative does not remain with the server as he rushes the net. A good return of serve can begin initiative reversal, and can result from a weak service, a strategical error on the part of the server, or an excellent shot by the receiver, in which case the serve was anticipated and a shot made good enough to cause the server to volley defensively.

The most effective return of serve to the "hard" Slice in this corner is down-the-line. The high speed factor that accompanies this serve causes many receivers to hit their return late. The down-the-line return utilizes this fact to best advantage, since hitting the

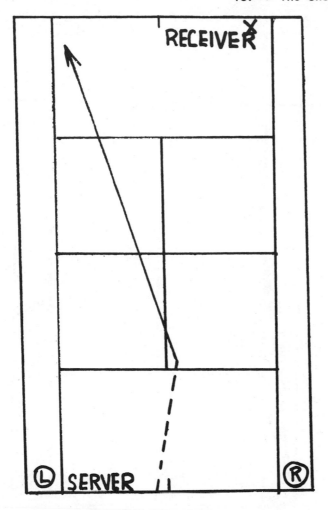

ball slightly late is an essential element of this stroke. When executed properly, the path of the ball never crosses in front of the server charging the net. This is of considerable advantage to the receiver since it eliminates much of the potential the net rusher has to hit from. The liabilities of this return include the fact that it will be received by the right-handed receiver's backhand, that much of the return's flight will travel over an area outside the playing surface, and that there is a relatively small margin for error between the netman's reach and the side line. As long as the down-the-line return is kept low and does not hang, it will pull the net-rushing server to the left side of the court when he makes his first volley. Given that his volley was a defensive response to a good service return, the server is now vulnerable to a passing shot to the right side

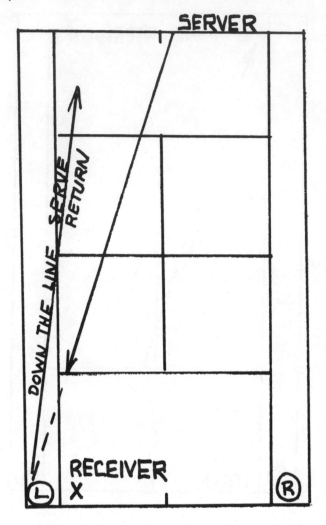

of the court. Passing shots are most effective with topspin since the spin induces the ball to dip below net level, but use of spin is not an absolute when the server has been pulled grossly out of position in his effort to volley the return of serve. In this case, the player should use his *most dependable* shot, since the critical element of the sequence, the service return, has already been made. Placement of the final passing shot to the right cannot be viewed as an absolute either, since it is useful also to hit behind the opponent who has anticipated the return but has committed himself too early. This is effectively used against the overeager netman or as a change of pace to discourage similar anticipation of future plays. By not varying their patterns of play, the opponent's anticipation indirectly forces many players into errors resulting from their attempt to make their shot better than is necessary to win the point. The smart player wins the point decisively but with as little risk as possible.

An alternative response to the down-the-line is crosscourt. While there is probably more percentage in this shot, it is difficult to hit against the hard Slice, since it must be received by the righthanded player's backhand and be contacted earlier, further in front, than the down-the-line. If the receiver is able to sufficiently compensate for these negative aspects of the shot, the crosscourt return has several notable assets. Primary among them is the diagonal flight of the ball across the court, and the fact that it crosses the lowest part of the net in the center. These characteristics make this alternative one with the percentages, and with a maximum margin for error.

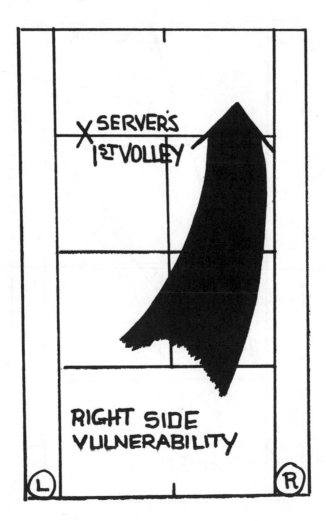

This return can become a distinct liability, however, if it hangs or crosses late in front of the server rushing the net. A circumstance such as this obviously reinforces the position of the server and makes the chances of initiative reversal considerably less. Once the ball passes this critical point of intersection with the path of the server as he rushes the net, it is a response that readily draws the server wide to the right side of the court. A significant aspect of this receiver sequence is the receiver's ability to quickly regain good defensive position in the center of the court, behind the baseline. It is imperative that the receiver compensate for the angle away from the court as quickly as possible, in order to be in good position to conclude the sequence after the server response to the crosscourt return. By pulling the server wide to the right, an area of vulnerabil-

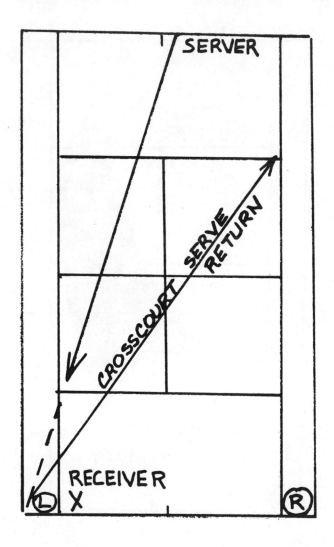

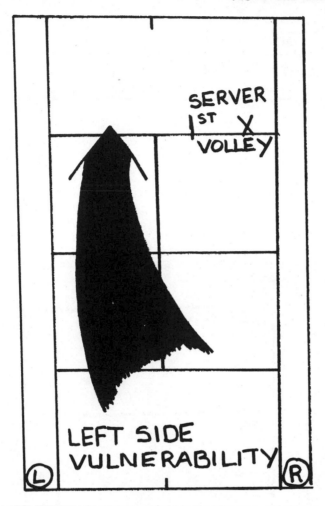

ity is created on the left side of the court, and it is to this position that the majority of the receiver's final passing shots should be directed. They should, however, again be interspersed with shots of variety in order to prevent the undue anticipation that can often detract from an otherwise good shot.

There are some theories of strategy and tactics that will always remain strikingly the same. We have already examined many of the different aspects that revolve around the spin, or lack of it, on the Cannonball and Slice services. These service spins are profound and very individual as they begin the server initiative, and the Topspin and American Twist remain no exception. A discussion of their effects and essential characteristics now follows.

9

THE TOPSPIN AND
AMERICAN TWIST SERVICES

OUTSIDE-CORNER DEUCE COURT

The American Twist service is used on the higher levels of play and

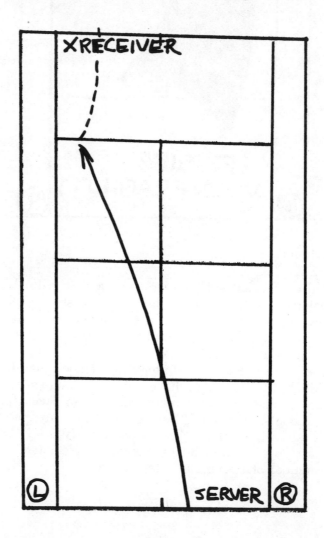

is characterized by excessive spin and irregular bounce. In order to achieve this spin one must contact the ball on its back side and brush over it at a diagonal from left to right. The Topspin serve, on the other hand, turns the ball straight over as its name correctly implies. This serve is hit harder and is often more aggressive due to this higher speed factor. The speed on this serve is generated not only by the inherent strength of the server's motion, but by the spin on the ball as well. This overspinning ball gives forth a positive force, separate and independent of any other part of the motion.

In order to apply any type of spin to the ball, it is necessary to avoid contacting the ball flush against the racket face. Spin is imparted to the tennis ball by grazing it in such a manner that only an edge of the ball actually hits the racket. This phenomenon is attained by creating an angle on the racket face in relation to the ball, and this is commonly done by serving with an Eastern backhand grip. Attainment of spin while using some other grip necessitates some type of physical variation or compensation in one's swing, in order to make up for the lack of natural angle on the racket face.

There are three grips commonly used in tennis today. They are the Eastern forehand and backhand, and the Continental. The im-

THE TOPSPIN SERVICE BRUSHES THE BALL ON ITS BACK SIDE AND TURNS IT STRAIGHT OVER

THE AMERICAN TWIST SERVE IS CHARACTERIZED BY A RATHER PECULIAR COMBINATION OF TOP AND SIDE SPIN

Western   Eastern Forehand   Continental   Eastern Backhand

portant thing to notice when studying these grips is angle of the racket face and how it changes with each grip. Such a study is imperative in any discussion of spin and how it is imparted to the ball. The Western grip is all but obsolete today, but it does represent an extreme in the angle progression toward the Eastern backhand. The more natural the angle one has to work from when serving, the more readily spin can be successfully applied to the ball. Note below how the angle of the racket face increases as one moves from the Western to Eastern backhand.

Any serve to the outside corner of the deuce court has the inherent disadvantage of being received by the righthanded player's forehand. The Slice however, should be considered an exception to the rule when executed properly since its slide to the left after the bounce pulls the receiver farther off the court, thereby negating the negative effect of being returned by the opponent's forehand.

The Topspin and American Twist services do not lead the opponent off the court when served to this corner. The Topspin serve bounces straight over and is characterized by a hop or kick that results from the rapid topspin turning the ball over. This serve is noted primarily for its speed and can be used effectively as a first or second delivery. It is valuable as a second serve since the spin allows for a reasonable degree of safety by pulling the ball down, into the service court, while still retaining much of its speed. The

American Twist, on the other hand, is characterized by an excessive spin factor and irregular bounce. This occurs as a result of its peculiar combination of topspin and slice, degrees of which vary with every serve. The degree of success one finds with either of these serves will depend to a large extent on how deep the ball bounces within the service court. If the serve is too short, the ball will spin out by the time it reaches the receiver, at which time much of its capacity to hinder the return of the opponent is lost. If kept deep, the receiver is forced to hit a high bouncing ball, the bounce and velocity of which are both erratic and unpredictable.

The fact that the spin of these serves does not pull the receiver further out of position after the ball bounces necessitates that the server accomplish this with his first volley. It is worth noting, however, that while the spin of these serves does not lead the receiver farther off the court, neither does it lead him to a more favorable position in center court. The server is directing his serve to an outside corner and, while it is not complemented by the spin-left of the Slice, it is noteworthy that the receiver must nevertheless retrieve it from an outside corner and position himself in the center

The slice serve curves away from the receiver.

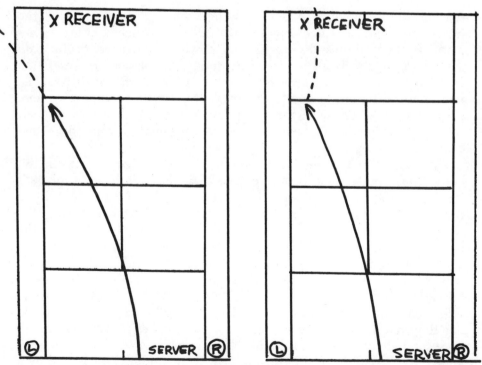

The kicking bounce of the twist bounces erratically toward the receiver.

of the court after his return. The server's first volley should logically be hit to the right side of the court and short, since the high bounce induced by the overspin on these serves has the effect of forcing the receiver back. The short volley adds a second dimension to the receiver's return since he must retrieve the ball not only from a position in the court widthwise to the right, but also depthwise, short. This added dimension forces the receiver to cover more ground and makes him vulnerable to several different winning placements behind him on the left. Whether one initiates this shot pattern by means of a forehand volley down-the-line or a backhand volley crosscourt, of course, depends upon the receiver's individual response to the service, and this will always vary.

If the receiver's response to the serve is defensive or above the level of the net, the net rusher should make his volley deep to the

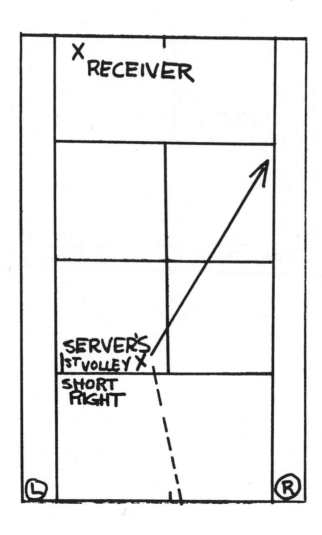

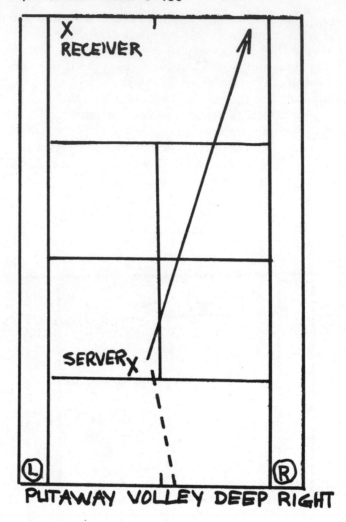

right side, rather than short. The deep volley is more decisive and consequently more likely to win the point than one short, the purpose of which is to pull the receiver out of position for a second and final volley.

Responses

The most obvious characteristics of the American Twist and Topspin services are that they have excessive overspin and high bounce. The effective response must, therefore, counter these characteristics. This is most effectively done by hitting the ball on the rise, before the spin can take full effect. To do this the receiver should position himself on, or inside, the baseline, and attack the

Putaway at the net via a lateral movement overhead smash. Note how the left hand across the body balances the forward motion of the swing.

A chipped return to the high bounce of the American twist service. Note the position inside the baseline.

serve before it reaches its height after the bounce. The fact that the ball does contain overspin necessitates that the receiver counter its action, and this is most commonly done with underspin, by chipping the return. This does not change the actual spin on the ball; rather it acknowledges and uses it to best advantage. It is very seldom that one sees a topspin serve returned with topspin. Such an action requires a complete reversal of the direction of the spin. Catching the ball early by hitting it on the rise has the positive effect of cutting down the time the server has to reach the net behind his serve. The chipped return to the net rusher's feet is an effective response to high-bouncing serves and often acts to reverse the initiative held by the server. Many players charge the net behind these serves, since the heavy spin has the effect of making the ball hang in the air longer, thereby giving the server more time to get from the baseline to the net. Hitting the return on the rise negates this advantage.

THE ACTUAL DIRECTION THAT THE BALL TURNS IS IDENTICAL FOR THE CHIPPED RETURN AND TOPSPIN SERVICE. RETURNING THE TOPSPIN SERVE WITH A TOPSPIN RETURN IS MORE DIFFICULT SINCE IT REQUIRES CHANGING THE DIRECTION THAT THE BALL IS TURNING.

The primary response pattern to this serve begins with a return of serve, usually chipped, crosscourt. This is the percentage return from this corner, since it crosses the center of the net, a portion that is six inches lower than either of the sides. The fact that the ball is in flight *across* the court allows for a comfortable margin for error from every dimension. It is also worth noting that the path of this return directly parallels the diagonal of the court, a distance that is longer than any within a rectangle. If executed properly, this return will be below the level of the net when it reaches the net rusher, thereby forcing him to volley up; an act that is decidedly defensive when compared to a volley hit above the net. The receiver's

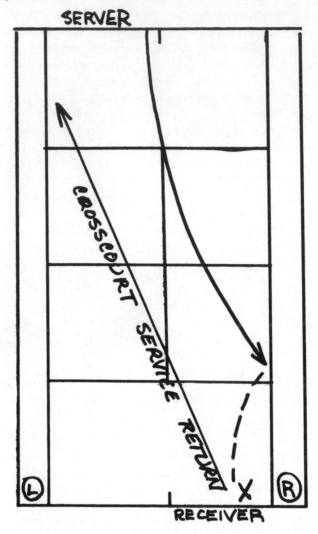

SERVER

CROSSCOURT SERVICE RETURN

Ⓛ   Ⓡ   X

RECEIVER

response to the first volley may be hit in numerous ways, all of which depend on the individual response to the low service return. If done successfully, the sequence of initiative reversal will have begun. The majority of the receiver's passing shots should be directed to the right side of the court, since the server had been drawn out of position to the left on the previous move. This, however, should be varied with shots back to the right, behind the opponent anticipating the more obvious passing shot to the left too early.

An alternative response when returning a serve from this position is down-the-line. This return is most effective since there is less actual distance from the impact point on the receiver's racket to

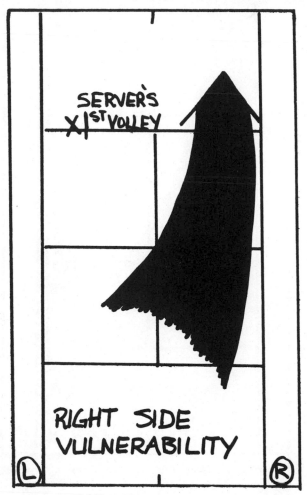

SERVER'S
X 1ST VOLLEY

RIGHT SIDE
VULNERABILITY

L   R

where the ball hits on the playing surface, as opposed to the cross-court, the path of which is a diagonal. The diagonal of any rectangle is longer than any of its sides. It should be noted that, while the crosscourt allows for greater distance, and consequently greater safety, it also requires more time for the ball to travel along such a path. Although there is less margin for error hitting down-the-line, it is a return that accumulates less time in flight than the crosscourt, thereby reaching its destination past the opponent quicker. Obviously, if the receiver hits the return on the rise and hits the return to the shortest alternative distancewise, one has the best chance of getting the ball past the server rushing the net. The receiver's passing shots should most often be directed to the left, since the down-the-line return pulled the server out of position right. However, patterns of

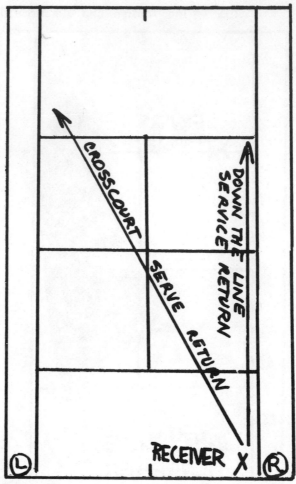

The down-the-line return covers less distance than the crosscourt, thereby getting past the server sooner.

play should always be varied in order to keep an opponent off balance. Lobs, shots of differing speeds and spins, as well as changes in direction, all have this desirable effect.

INSIDE-CORNER DEUCE COURT

When served to the deuce court, the Topspin and Twist services are most favorably hit to the inside corner. This is true primarily because the ball will be received by the righthanded player's backhand. The fact that the backhand is the weaker side on many levels of player competence makes use of an unpredictable spinning serve such as the Twist very appropriate. The harder Topspin is useful when served to the backhand as well, since it is characterized by a

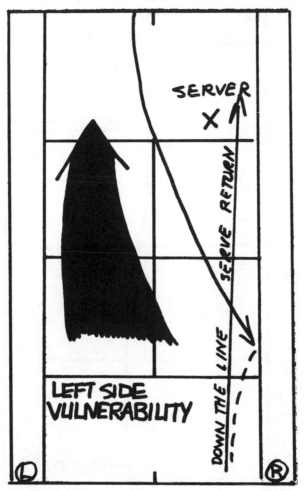

high-speed factor that is complemented by the rapid overspin kick. The receiver had natural angle to work from when drawn wide of the court, while retrieving the ball served to the outside corner, and could potentially hit his return down-the-line or crosscourt with considerably less effort. The receiver must create his own angle when retrieving a serve down the center. The fact that the receiver has no angle to work from often leaves the net-rushing server with a similar problem since, in many cases, adjustment to the spin becomes the primary concern of the receiver, thereby causing the ball to be hit without conscious direction back down the middle. The receiver will readily position himself in the center of the court since receiving the serve from an inside corner necessarily brings him toward such a position. The fact that the receiver is in good position makes it wise for the server to volley

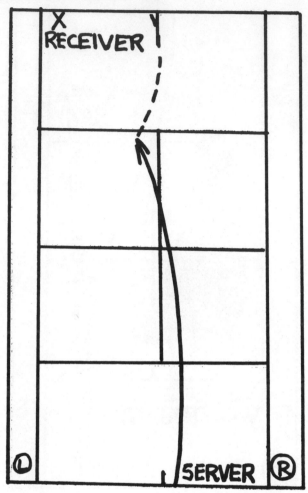

his first shot crosscourt, regardless of whether he receives it as a forehand or backhand volley. The short crosscourt volley does as much damage as any to an opponent in good defensive position, since it makes him vulnerable from two separate court dimensions, length and width. Thus the receiver is not only pulled across the court but inside it as well. This is an excellent combination because one may successfully volley the opponent's return away, not only to the opposite side of the court, but behind him as well.

The experienced player anticipates shots in succession since it is a fact that certain initiatives repeatedly elicit very similar responses. Knowing this, one should shade to the side of the court that one hit the first volley, in order to station oneself in proper position for the next shot. This allows the server to effectively cut off the receiver's

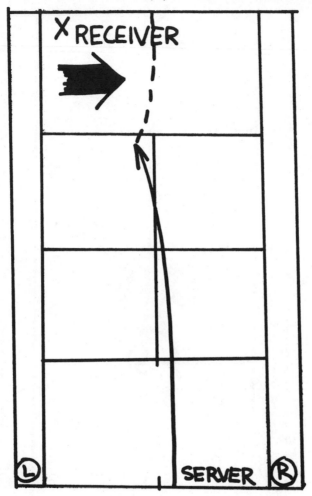

response to his first volley. This act substantially reduces the potential angle of the opponent's return, and is an essential element of any shot sequence, since without it the receiver is left with a more favorable angle from which to hit his passing shot.

There are times when one has the opportunity to put the first volley away and this should be done when the return of serve is weak and above net level. The side of the court one directs the put-away volley will vary and depend directly on the receiver's response to the serve and the net rusher's estimation of the opponent's vulnerability at the time. In most cases, it is to the server's advantage to keep such a shot deep, since any ball hit close to the baseline limits, substantially, the play available to the receiver after the bounce.

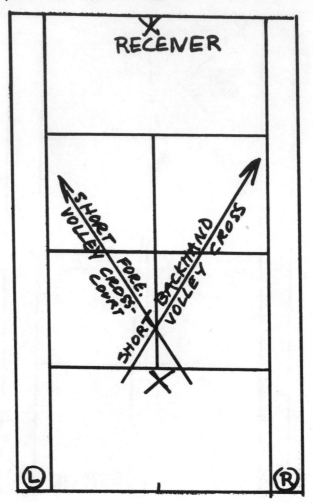

Responses

In order to reverse the initiative held by the server, one must catch the kicking serve on the rise, as soon after the bounce as possible. These serves carry so much spin when executed properly, that they tend to hang and arch as they cross the net. The ball remains in the air longer than a serve hit on a line more directly into the service court. Consequently, catching the ball on the rise when receiving it tends to compensate for the additional time the server has to follow into good position at the net, while at the same time allowing the receiver to play the serve before the spin takes full effect. The longer one waits to receive these serves, especially the Twist, the more pronounced the action from the spin will be.

The crosscourt service return is again an excellent response to

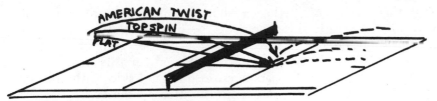

THE TYPICAL ARCH AND KICK OF THE AMERICAN
TWIST, TOPSPIN, AND FLAT SERVES

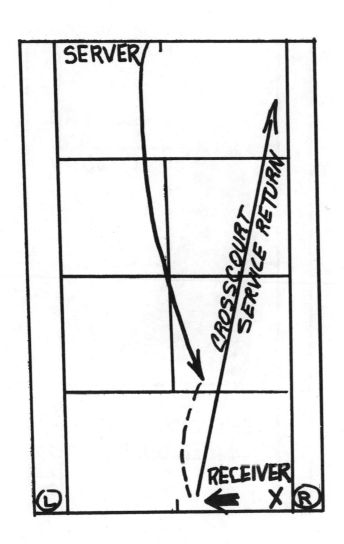

either of these serves. Whether a shot is considered crosscourt or down-the-line is directly dependent on the position of the player executing the shot and has no direct bearing on the path of the ball in relation to the court. A crosscourt backhand, in this instance, is the shot that passes from the backhand to forehand side of the player hitting the ball, regardless of his or her position on the court.

The crosscourt return from this position is an excellent return because it never passes in front of the server rushing the net. As was the case with the forehand down-the-line from the outside corner, this ball covers less actual distance than a return that travels diagonally across the court. This fact, plus catching the ball on the rise, makes the probability high that the receiver will be able to get the ball past the server before he is in adequate position to make his

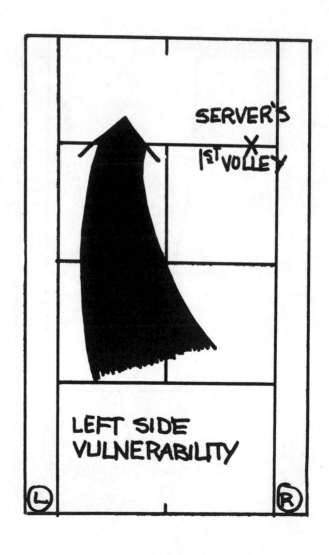

first volley. While this is an ideal return, its difficulty should be noted; for, as with the forehand down-the-line, there is less area necessary to hit, as well as the net being a very significant six inches higher on the sides.

The manner in which the server responds to this return depends on how good the service return is, in terms of speed and placement, as well as how adequately the server is able to cover the sideline with his volley. It is not unusual to draw a defensive return from this shot, and one should be prepared to play it quickly, sometimes even with a volley, while the server is still out of position. Many players lacking such preparation find themselves attempting to make this final passing shot better than necessary, indirectly forcing themselves into unneeded errors. The forcing shot of this sequence was

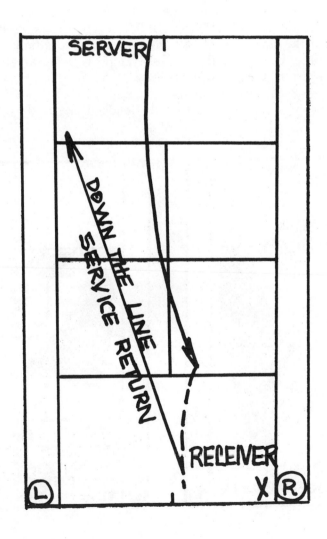

the service return and, while the passing shot completes the sequence, it is not the primary agent. This passing shot is most often directed to the left side of the court, since the successful service return pulled the server wide to the right. However, no sequence should be repeated continuously. Patterns of play should be varied so as to avoid any undue anticipation on the part of the server.

An alternative to the crosscourt in this corner is a return down-the-line. This shot is considered down-the-line because the path of the ball does not pass from one side of the man executing the shot to the other. The ball is hit on his left and remains on that side, thereby making it down-the-line. Shots of great angle are not an exclusive trait of the crosscourt return, and the down-the-line service return from the inside corner of the deuce court is an excellent case in point. Since the flight of this ball passes in front of the server rushing the net, it is desirable that this shot not only be one of considerable angle, but also be short, thereby reaching its destination before the server reaches a good volleying position. This is the same shot one uses in doubles, where angle is necessary to keep the ball away from the opposing netman. As mentioned earlier, the chipped service return is the most common when receiving a high bouncing spin serve, since it readily lends itself to the return of a

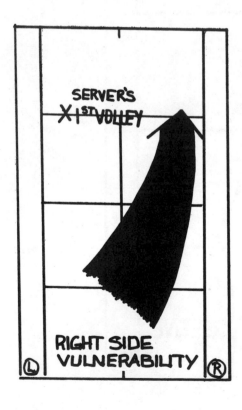

RIGHT SIDE
VULNERABILITY

HITTING BEHIND THE
OPPONENT REVEALING
HIS ANTICIPATION OF THE
RIGHT SIDE OPENING
TOO EARLY

ball on the rise, thereby cutting down the time the server has to reach the net for good volleying position. The backspin on the ball gives the receiver an additional amount of control that makes it possible to direct the return low over the net and with forcing angle.

As was the case with the crosscourt return, the direction of the final passing shot will depend totally on how and where the server's response to the service return is directed. The obvious opening is to the right side of the court, since the return of serve pulled the server wide to the left. It is wise to vary any pattern of play, however, by hitting behind the opponent revealing his anticipation too soon, and with lobs over his head.

INSIDE-CORNER ADD COURT

Any serve to this corner has the inherent disadvantage of being

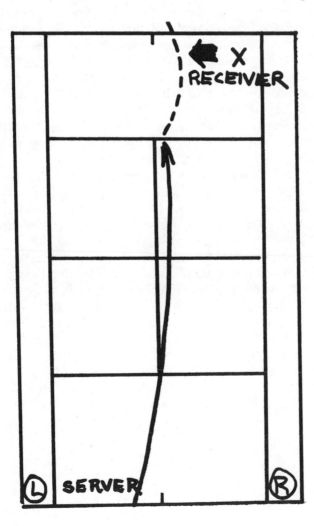

received by the righthanded player's forehand. These serves do not have the advantage of the spin-induced slide left witnessed in the Slice, since the nature of overspin causes the ball to kick up and out, thus forcing the receiver to return the service off of a difficult high bounce. The Topspin serve, characterized more for its speed than excess spin, is effectively used to this corner because the distance from the server to the impact point in the service court is less to any inside corner. This in effect, adds to the speed of the serve since the sooner the ball reaches the receiver, the harder it is considered. With the exception of the left-handed player or one with a peculiar inability with respect to receiving spin on the forehand, these serves are most effectively used as "serves of variety." The wise server will always change his services, both in type and corner direction, in an attempt to keep the receiver off balance and to prevent the undue anticipation mentioned previously.

Because the serve will be received by most opponents' stronger side, the forehand, the server will not always be presented with a totally defensive return. He will, however, find quite a few returns hit back down the middle. This stems from the fact that serves to any inside corner leave the receiver without angle to hit from; and most players are unwilling to attempt a shot of unusual angle when caught receiving an unexpected serve. Adjustment to the kick of either of these serves is a job in itself, especially on the higher levels of play where these serves are constantly kept deep in the service court. When and if the service return is hit back down the middle, the server can be said to have retained the initiative to that point. Just as the down-the-middle shot limited the angle for the receiver, the server is likewise presented with the same problem when he encounters the service return back down the center from the receiver. He must create angle with his volley and this is most easily done crosscourt. Whether the crosscourt return is executed as a forehand or backhand volley is, of course, totally dependent on the direction of the receiver's service return. The *short* crosscourt volley does as much damage as any as far as pulling a man away from the center of the court. The following statement by the immortal Bill Tilden illustrates the significance as well as the fundamentality of this point since Tilden's reign in tennis during the 1920's occurred before the emergence of the so-called big game theory so prevalent today. "No longer will consistently deep driving prove a satisfactory standard. Today (the 1920's) one must vary distance as well as direction."[1] The manner in which the receiver reacts to such a volley

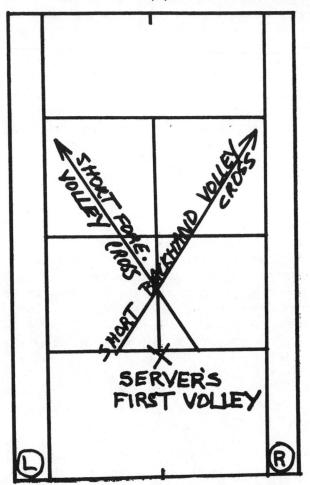

will always vary with relation to his individual abilities and judgment of the situation at hand. However, the server can limit the choices available to the receiver by shading to the side of the court the first volley crosscourt was hit, thereby dissecting the potential percentage angle of the receiver's return. Having drawn the receiver into the court with the short first volley, the server is now in a position to end the point with a deep volley to the opposite side, behind him. The forcing shot of this sequence was the first volley, a shot that successfully moved the receiver into a vulnerable position for the final putaway.

When one encounters a high or defensive return of serve, a conscious effort should be made to put the ball away, ending the point outright. This is most commonly done with a deep volley to either corner. A deep shot close to the baseline is more decisive in the putaway sequence because it limits the play of the ball after the bounce much more than a shot of less depth that bounces in front and to the opponent, consequently allowing for a possible return.

Responses

The righthanded player has his best chance of reversing the initiative held by the server when he receives service from this corner. The forehand is a stronger shot for most players than the backhand, with the likes of Ken Rosewall, of course, being a notable exception. Receiving the ball from an inside corner leads the receiver into an ideal defensive position in the center of the court, a fact that subsequently allows him to follow the forcing service return with a more or less unhurried passing shot. While it is true that a service to an inside corner forces the receiver to create his own angle on his return, it is also true that he has his best chance of doing exactly that off of his forehand side. Through close observation of the server's toss, the experienced receiver will notice early that one of the kicking serves is coming. When he sees the toss over the server's head, he quickly moves inside the baseline and prepares to return the serve on the rise, as soon after the bounce as possible. Such a move not only allows the receiver to play the ball before the full effect of the spin is felt, but also cuts down, significantly, the time the server has to reach good volleying position at the net. Accomplishing this by catching the server as he crosses "no man's land" in the middle of the court does as much as anything to insure the ultimate success of the service return.

The most ideal service return in this corner is crosscourt. It has many of the same characteristics that were discussed with respect to the crosscourt return from the inside corner of the deuce court except that, as mentioned before, it has the rather distinct receiver advantage of being returned by the righthander's forehand.

As mentioned before, it is always to the advantage of the receiver to always attack the kicking serve on the rise. Attacking a service, however, should not be misinterpreted to mean slugging the return. Rather, the criterion for such a judgment should be based upon the positive or negative effect the shot has on the opponent's subsequent shot. Such an axiom is particularly relevant with respect to heavily spin-laden balls where overcoming the effect of spin through the use of additional pace is most impractical. Hitting the serve on the rise is most effectively done by moving inside the baseline, in an effort to catch it as soon after the bounce as possible. With these serves, one is faced with the additional problem of controlling the kicking action of the spin, most commonly done with the use of a backspin chip shot. It is very unusual to see a player completely reverse the direction of the spin imparted by the serve, in this case returning

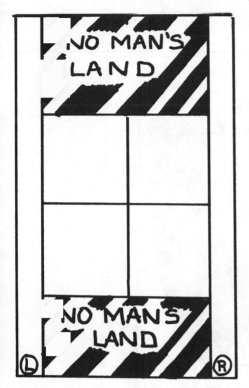

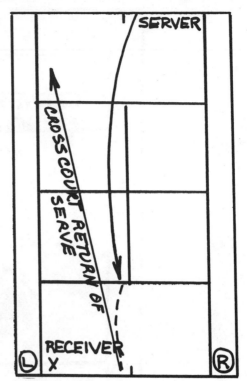

an overspinning serve with a topspin return. Thus, the wise receiver does not seek to change the spin itself but only its action effect. When viewed pictorially, one immediately recognizes that the Topspin serve hit by player A has induced the ball to spin in the same direction as would the backspin shot of player B receiving it. In this light, it is wise to play the spin as it comes to you. Spin reversal is impractical and unlikely to succeed a favorable percentage of the time. (See page 153 for illustration.)

Having pulled the server wide to the left side of the court, with the crosscourt return, the logical opening for the receiver's passing shot is back to the right. How easily one is able to accomplish this depends on how the server reacts to his opponent's return of serve. The service return is the forcing shot of this sequence and it is at this point that initiative reversal begins. While the majority of one's passing shots should be directed to the opening created to the right, occasional shots should also be hit back to the left, behind the opponent. Undue anticipation can negate much of the effect of even the most perfect execution. It is useful that the opponent be made aware that you are always weighing different alternatives and that you are never playing according to tactical absolutes.

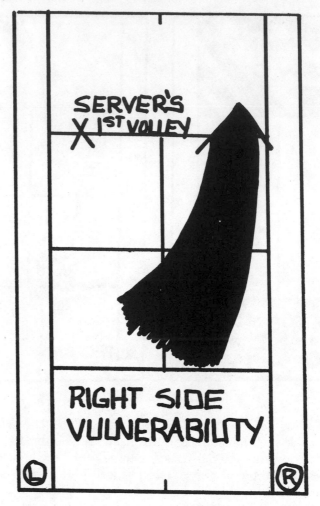

The return of serve down-the-line is an alternative response to the crosscourt. This return is much the same as one used in doubles from this same court, where down-the-line angle is necessary in order to keep the ball away from the opposing netman. It is useful to hit this return as soon as possible, since the flight of the return passes in front of the server once he is in position at the net. It is obviously to one's advantage for the ball to cross this point in its flight before the server arrives in a position to volley it aggressively. Once this is accomplished, the angle of the return will draw the server wide right in his attempt to cover it. Such a response leaves open an area of vulnerability on the left side of the court, where the majority of one's passing shots should be directed. Again, the service return acted as the forcing shot of this sequence, since it was this shot that opened the court for the final passing shot.

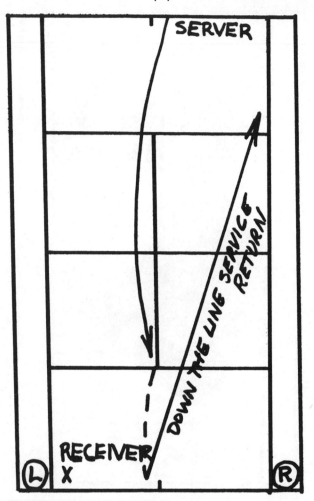

OUTSIDE-CORNER ADD COURT

The Topspin and American Twist services can be used very effectively to this corner. When served deep in the service court, adjustment to the erratic bounce of the Twist is a dominant factor. The serve necessarily drives the receiver off the court, as well as requiring play by the righthanded player's weaker side, the backhand. This is a most effective combination and one that has been proven repeatedly. Couple this with the fact that the Twist tends to hang in the air longer than any other serve and one has a service combination that is likely to force a weak or defensive response while allowing the server a maximum amount of time to assume a good volleying position at the net. The Topspin serve, characterized

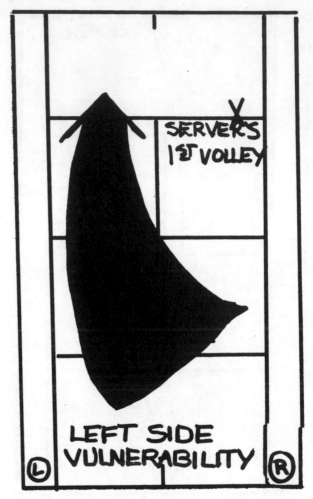

primarily by its speed, can be used effectively to this corner as well. The server, similarly, not only forces the receiver off the court with a naturally aggressive serve, but also forces him on his weaker side.

The potential percentage angle of an opponent's next shot has been mentioned before in this section, and it is of no less significance here. It is wise to shade to the right side of the court, in this instance, since the serve has driven the receiver to that side of the court for his return. The apex of the angle, therefore, will be at the point, off the court to the right, that he contacts the ball. A defensive return is as likely to occur in this sequence as any and one should be prepared to end the point outright if given the chance. Such a volley should be directed deep to the left side of the court since the receiver has been pulled wide right. It is important to hit

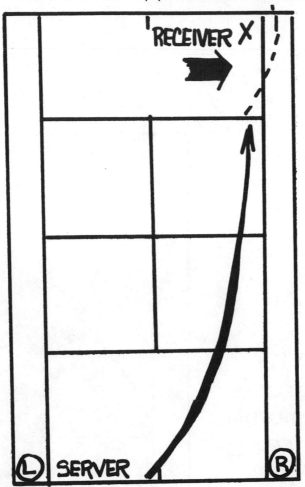

the volley deep since the added depth limits significantly any play of the ball after the bounce. A short ball, on the other hand, bounces in front of the opponent, consequently leaving more potential for a return.

Should the service return be more aggressive, and this often occurs when the serve bounces shallow in the court, one's first volley should be placed short to the left side of the court. Whether this is accomplished by means of a forehand volley crosscourt or backhand down-the-line is dependent on how and where the receiver's return is directed, and this will always vary. Close observation has revealed that the crosscourt forehand is easier because of the inherent difficulty of returning *any* crosscourt shot down-the-line. Such a shot requires very good timing and excellent body position. Any ball

NOTE DISSECTION
OF THE POTENTIAL
ANGLE OF RECEIVER'S
RETURN

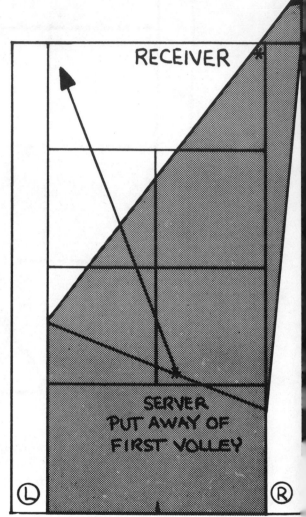

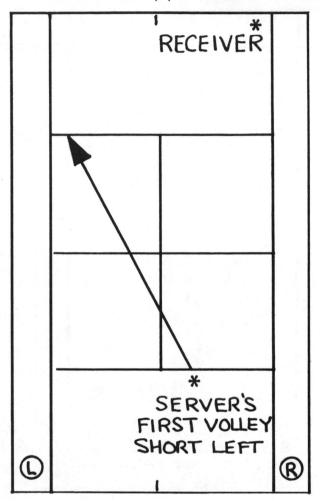

hit down-the-line requires more of a closed stance (turned more sideways) than the crosscourt, the stance of which can be more open and facing the net, since contacting the ball slightly more in front is an essential element of the stroke execution. The contradiction occurs when one is presented with a ball coming from a crosscourt corner that one must direct down-the-line from a closed stance. Inexperienced players attempt to make this shot through some type of body compensation, usually with the wrist, but very few find any consistent success. Nevertheless volleying the ball short has the positive effect of drawing the opponent inside the playing area, a position that is rather precarious, setting the stage for a final volley behind him to the right.

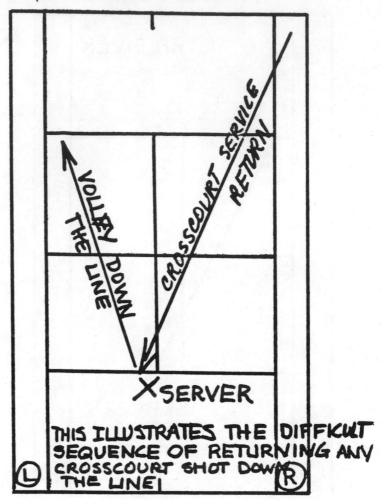

Responses

The ideal response to the kicking serves in this corner is down-the-line. Such a return will not pass in front of the server coming to the net, thereby eliminating much of his potential to hit a successful volley. By not crossing the court, however, the shot must be made with considerably more precision, since there is a relatively small margin for error between the sideline and the server's reach. In this light, it must be considered a shot against the percentages and one to be played when one is in a position to afford the chance. World-class competitors will attempt this shot from the outside corners more often since they, in essence, play sets to gain but one service break; and it is a fact that the conservative shot rarely wins on this level of play. Various responses to a forcing return will be en-

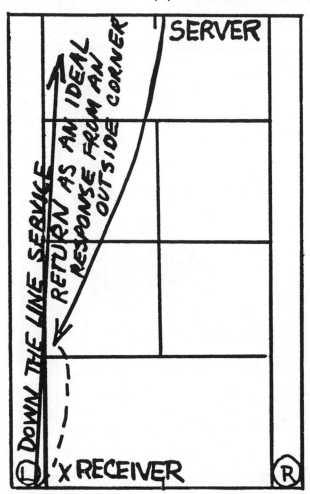

countered, and they will always be individual and with direct relation to the server's ability to cover the shot in question. This return
pulls the server wide to the left, thereby creating an area of vulnerability to the right and it is to this area that the majority of one's
passing shots should be directed. The aggressive return was the
forcing shot of the sequence, as it set the stage for the server's final
downfall and loss of the initiative.

The crosscourt return is valuable from this corner, also, and is
complemented by the fact that the receiver contacts the ball wide
of the court. Such a position presents the receiver with maximum
angle from which to hit his shot. One should catch the ball as soon
after the bounce as possible, contacting the ball adequately in
front to direct it crosscourt. Hitting the ball early after the bounce

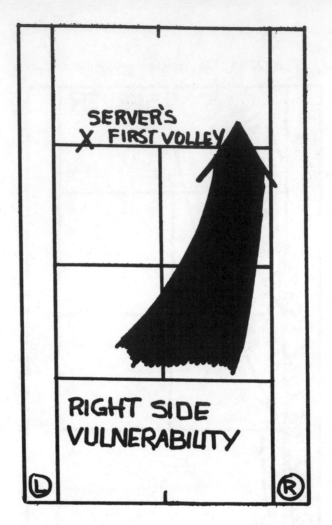

SERVER'S
X FIRST VOLLEY

RIGHT SIDE
VULNERABILITY

Ⓛ   Ⓡ

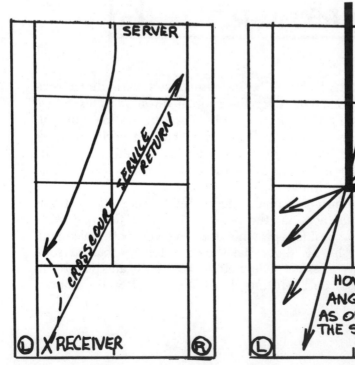

SERVER

CROSSCOURT SERVICE RETURN

Ⓛ   X RECEIVER   Ⓡ

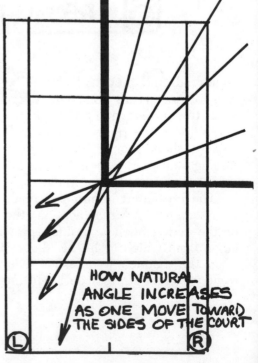

HOW NATURAL
ANGLE INCREASES
AS ONE MOVE TOWARD
THE SIDES OF THE COURT

Ⓛ   Ⓡ

has the secondary effect of limiting the time the server has to reach the net, a fact that is important when one considers the necessity of getting the ball across the server's path before he reaches an adequate volleying position. When executed properly, the crosscourt angle will draw the server wide to the right side of the court, thereby creating an area of vulnerability to the left. It is to this opening that the majority of one's passing shots should be directed. The receiver can prevent much of the play on this shot by the server by successfully eliminating any undue amount of anticipation. The wise player seeks to always keep his opponent off balance and unaware of the direction of his next shot. This is often accomplished with shots back to the right, away from the more obvious opening to the left, and with lobs over the server's head.

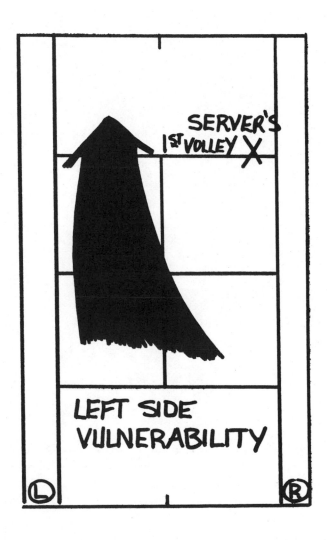

Part III. The Systems-Analysis Concept: Performance Objectification

The impact of technology and scientific thinking has spread into the realm of sport. The 1972 Olympic Games lent support to thought that the days of informal judgments of athletic accomplishment are over worldwide and in virtually all sports. Tape measures and manual timing devices have disappeared, with one Olympic swimming event hanging on the difference of 1/1000 of a second measured by a computer. While tennis was not a part of the Olympics, it is apparent that off-the-cuff advice from pros and coaches is no longer an adequate training device. The *Tennis Player's Profile* and *Player Interaction Analysis* have filled this void in the game of tennis, and a discussion of their essential characteristics and practical applications now follows.

These new systems of evaluation have been referred to as "the first scientific systems analysis of individual tennis performance." The term *systems analysis* is often used to identify different self-contained systems. Close observation has shown that there is a very real difference between random play in tennis, one shot at a time, and play that occurs in patterns. "Some players are accustomed to handling certain shots in a stereotyped manner. They may always return a crosscourt drive with a similar shot, if on the backhand side, for instance; or they may invariably drive down the line on the forehand side, or lob from a fast drive if in the extreme backhand corner; or form some other forced habit."[1] Tennis players, as well as people in general, are much more predictable than is commonly believed. These methods of objectifying player performance tell how many patterns the charted player is using, how effectively, and how appropriately. Such an analysis allows the player and/or coach to define dominant stroke types; a much more sophisticated approach than the shallow, but very common, observation that an opponent's backhand might be weaker than his forehand. These repeated patterns of play are "subsystems" of a tennis match, and the profile chart is a "systems analysis". From this innovation, it is now possible to observe and criticize player performance in terms of aggressive patterns of play, repeated errors, and patterns of omission—those shots that should have been used but weren't.

When composing these systems, a way had to be found to cate-

---

1. J. P. Peret, *Psychology of Advanced Play in Lawn Tennis,* The Lawn Tennis Library, Vol III (New York: American Lawn Tenis, Inc., 1929), p. 33.

MATCH NUMBER _____ DATE _____

STROKE KEY

T - TOPSPIN	d - DEEP
C - CHIPPED	S - SHORT
F - FLAT	O - CIRCLE ANY
L - LOB	PUTAWAY OR
D - DROP SHOT	FORCED ERROR

TENNIS PLAYER'S PROFILE   TENNIS COACH'S COMMENTS:

NAME - _____ LEFT or RIGHT
OPPONENT- _____ LEFT or RIGHT
COMPOSITE PROFILE SCORE _____
MATCH SCORE _____
COURT SURFACE _____

SCORING VALUES

+2 ANY PUTAWAY SHOT OR FORCED ERROR
+1 ANY AGGRESSIVE SHOT
-O- DOWN THE MIDDLE OR DEFENSIVE SHOT
-1 ANY ERROR

STROKE PROFILE

| FOREHAND | BACKHAND | FOREHAND SERVE RETURN | BACKHAND SERVE RETURN | FOREHAND VOLLEY | BACKHAND VOLLEY | OVERHEAD SMASH |

Row labels:
- AGGRESSIVE CROSS COURT +1
- AGGRESSIVE DOWN THE LINE +1
- DOWN THE MIDDLE -O-
- DEFENSIVE -O-
- ERRORS LONG -1
- ERRORS WIDE -1
- ERRORS NETTED -1

TOTAL (per column)

SERVICE PROFILE

Row labels:
- FIRST SERVES
- ACES +2
- EFFECTIVE FLAT +1
- EFFECTIVE TWIST +1
- EFFECTIVE SLICE +1
- SHORT SERVES -O-
- FAULTS LONG -1
- FAULTS NETTED -1
- FAULTS WIDE OUTSIDE -1
- FAULTS WIDE INSIDE -1
- DOUBLE FAULTS -2

SERVICE COMPETENCE TOTAL

© CRAIG R. WILSON   1972

PLAYER INTER-ACTION ANALYSIS

SET NUMBER _____ DATE _____

POINT BREAKDOWN NOTED BY ANY NUMBER
ENTERED IN ERROR COLUMNS OR BY A
CIRCLE DENOTING A PUTAWAY.

GAME SCORE	
1	1
2	2
3	3
4	4
5	5
6	6
7	7

SCORING VALUES

+2 ANY PUTAWAY SHOT
+1 ANY AGGRESSIVE SHOT
-0- DOWN THE MIDDLE OR DEFENSIVE SHOT
-1 ANY ERROR

PLAYER A _____ LEFT RIGHT PLAYER B _____ LEFT RIGHT
MATCH SCORE _____ MATCH SCORE _____
ANALYSIS SCORE _____ ANALYSIS SCORE _____
COURT SURFACE _____ COURT SURFACE _____
EVENT _____ EVENT _____

COMMENTS:

SERVICE PROFILE

PLAYER A   PLAYER B

FIRST SERVES
ACES +2
EFFECTIVE FLAT +1
EFFECTIVE TWIST +1
EFFECTIVE SLICE +1
SHORT SERVES -0-
FAULTS LONG -1
FAULTS NETTED -1
FAULTS WIDE OUTSIDE -1
FAULTS WIDE INSIDE -1
DOUBLE FAULTS -2

SERVICE COMPETENCE TOTALS

STROKE PROFILE

FOREHAND   BACKHAND   FOREHAND SERVE RETURN   BACKHAND SERVE RETURN   FOREHAND VOLLEY   BACKHAND VOLLEY   OVERHEAD SMASH

AGGRESSIVE CROSS COURT +1
AGGRESSIVE DOWN THE LINE +1
DOWN THE MIDDLE -0-
DEFENSIVE -0-
ERRORS LONG -1
ERRORS WIDE -1
ERRORS NETTED -1

A B TOTAL

© CRAIG R. WILSON 1972
ALL RIGHTS RESERVED

TENNIS PLAYER'S PROFILE — TENNIS COACH'S COMMENTS:

MATCH NUMBER _____ DATE _____

STROKE KEY

T - TOPSPIN	d - DEEP
C - CHIPPED	S - SHORT
F - FLAT	O - CIRCLE ANY
L - LOB	PUTAWAY OR
D - DROP SHOT	FORCED ERROR

NAME - _____ LEFT or RIGHT
OPPONENT- _____ LEFT or RIGHT
COMPOSITE PROFILE SCORE _____
MATCH SCORE _____
COURT SURFACE _____

SCORING VALUES

+2 ANY PUTAWAY SHOT OR FORCED ERROR
+1 ANY AGGRESSIVE SHOT
-0- DOWN THE MIDDLE OR DEFENSIVE SHOT
-1 ANY ERROR

STROKE PROFILE

	FOREHAND	BACKHAND	FOREHAND SERVE RETURN	BACKHAND SERVE RETURN	FOREHAND VOLLEY	BACKHAND VOLLEY	OVERHEAD SMASH
AGGRESSIVE CROSS COURT +1							
AGGRESSIVE DOWN THE LINE +1							
DOWN THE MIDDLE -0-							
DEFENSIVE -0-							
ERRORS LONG -1							
ERRORS WIDE -1							
ERRORS NETTED -1							
	TOTAL	TOTAL	TOTAL	TOTAL	TOTAL	TOTAL	TOTAL

SERVICE PROFILE

FIRST SERVES	
ACES +2	
EFFECTIVE FLAT +1	
EFFECTIVE TWIST +1	
EFFECTIVE SLICE +1	
SHORT SERVES -0-	
FAULTS LONG -1	
FAULTS NETTED -1	
FAULTS WIDE OUTSIDE -1	
FAULTS WIDE INSIDE -1	
DOUBLE FAULTS -2	
SERVICE COMPETENCE TOTAL	

© CRAIG R. WILSON 1972

MATCH NUMBER _____ DATE _____

STROKE KEY

T - TOPSPIN	d - DEEP
C - CHIPPED	S - SHORT
F - FLAT	O - CIRCLE ANY
L - LOB	PUTAWAY OR
D - DROP SHOT	FORCED ERROR

TENNIS PLAYER'S PROFILE   TENNIS COACH'S COMMENTS:

NAME - _____ LEFT or RIGHT _____
OPPONENT - _____ LEFT or RIGHT _____
COMPOSITE PROFILE SCORE _____
MATCH SCORE _____
COURT SURFACE _____

SCORING VALUES

+2 ANY PUTAWAY SHOT OR
    <u>FORCED ERROR</u>
+1 ANY AGGRESSIVE SHOT
-0- DOWN THE MIDDLE OR
    DEFENSIVE SHOT
-1 ANY ERROR

STROKE PROFILE

	FOREHAND	BACKHAND	FOREHAND SERVE RETURN	BACKHAND SERVE RETURN	FOREHAND VOLLEY	BACKHAND VOLLEY	OVERHEAD SMASH
AGGRESSIVE CROSS COURT +1							
AGGRESSIVE DOWN THE LINE +1							
DOWN THE MIDDLE -0-							
DEFENSIVE -0-							
ERRORS LONG -1							
ERRORS WIDE -1							
ERRORS NETTED -1							
TOTAL	TOTAL	TOTAL	TOTAL	TOTAL	TOTAL	TOTAL	TOTAL

SERVICE PROFILE

FIRST SERVES	
ACES +2	
EFFECTIVE FLAT +1	
EFFECTIVE TWIST +1	
EFFECTIVE SLICE +1	
SHORT SERVES -0-	
FAULTS LONG -1	
FAULTS NETTED -1	
FAULTS WIDE OUTSIDE -1	
FAULTS WIDE INSIDE -1	
DOUBLE FAULTS -2	
SERVICE COMPETENCE TOTAL	

© CRAIG R. WILSON   1972

MATCH NUMBER _____   DATE _____

	STROKE KEY	
T - TOPSPIN	d - DEEP	
C - CHIPPED	S - SHORT	
F - FLAT	O - CIRCLE ANY	
L - LOB	PUTAWAY OR	
D - DROP SHOT	FORCED ERROR	

gorize all of the strokes, all of the alternatives of placement, as well as the various characteristics that describe the ball as hit by one of these strokes. The strokes include the serve, forehand, backhand, forehand service return, backhand service return, forehand volley, backhand volley, and overhead smash. The alternatives of placement are crosscourt, down-the-line, down-the-middle, errors long, errors wide, and errors netted. The stroke characteristics that are abbreviated and inserted into the chart's small squares are defensive, lob, dropshot, topspin, chipped, flat, deep, and short (shallow). The variety of serves includes the American Twist, Slice, and Flat. The descriptive information on these service alternatives is good first serves, aces, short (within the service court), faults long, faults netted, faults wide inside, faults wide outside, and double faults. In essence, the *Tennis Player's Profile* and *Player Interaction Analysis* are tools that allow one to quickly and accurately record thirty-three different categories of information in a form the player or his coach can readily interpret. The next two chapters explain these two instruments in detail and illustrate their practical application.

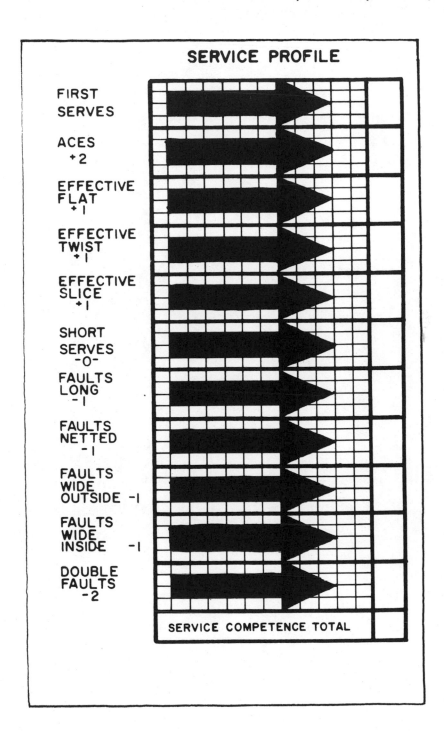

10

THE TENNIS PLAYER'S PROFILE

The *Tennis Player's Profile* is designed for use on one player and seeks to describe one player's reactions and initiatives on the tennis court. There is a place for every player's behavior on the chart, and once a thorough familiarity with the *Profile* layout is attained, the charting task can be enjoyable and interesting, as the patterns of play evolve throughout the match. The numerical system underlying the *Profile* rewards aggressive play (+1), neither punishes nor rewards neutral play (–0–), and punishes negative erroring performance (−1). Much of the significance of the system stems from the fact that it evaluates and rewards numerically the adequacy of a player's actual stroke performance. It is biased toward aggressive shot making in order to encourage the development of the aggressive style of play necessary to compete successfully in tournament tennis today. Every shot is recorded, with errors negating aggressive shots, thus allowing for a total score, stroke by stroke, as well as in total, after addition and cancellation at the conclusion of the match. In this way, the player is able to receive a totally objective criticism of his actual play, irrespective of set and match scores.

Like all good tools, the *Tennis Player's Profile* is flexible. It works with personal self-paced learning, formal individual instruction, as well as the systematic coaching of competitive teams. Because the system is weighted to favor the aggressive play witnessed on the higher levels of competition, a close correlation between player victories and high *Profile* scores can be seen. There are exceptions, however, and they occur when, for example, a highly developed maintenance type player encounters an ineffectual, overly cautious, or faulting aggressive player. Both of these particular playing styles have their own distinctive advantages and peculiar liabilities, and changing from one pattern to another, even though of long-term value, may lead to temporary setbacks as far as winning and losing matches is concerned. The *Tennis Player's Profile* is an aid in coaching young players for tournament competition since it rewards aggressive play alone. Merely keeping the ball in play does not score. It trains a player to think aggressively, play aggressively, and concentrate one hundred percent of the time, while knowing that every lazy shot, as

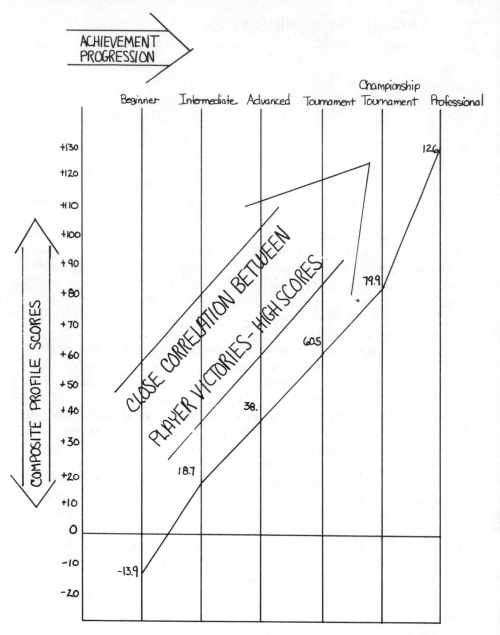

well as every good shot, is being recorded, and that it influences total *Profile* score. Students learn to take pride in their charted performances since they are, in essence, playing against themselves and whatever their potential achievement level may be. Winning a set or match in this experience is still important, but the development of a personal style of high quality is even more so. As a tool, the *Profile* contributes a wealth of information about all of the performance subsystems that contribute to or detract from victory on the courts. In essence, game and set scores have always revealed WHO won—now it is possible to document WHY.

This system should be used anywhere intensive coaching is taking place, whether by the pro, at a tennis camp, by players grading each other or scouting an opponent. The *Profile* does not attempt to make all players alike. Rather it reveals a player's total pattern of behavior and lets him decide how to remain individualistic and still achieve increasingly better results. When compiled as a notebook, the *Profile* shows the career progress of a student and parallels a case history showing individual patterns of play in relation to an entire career. It shows the individual player performance as a slowly evolving process, occasionally rapid, but often erratic with periodic slumps and plateaus. A more specific discussion of the data accumulated up until this time now follows.

THE DATA

While the data on *Profile* scores has not been accumulated over an extremely long period of time, enough has been compiled to draw some rather definite conclusions. The correlation between high *Profile* scores and high achievement level has already been noted and seen on the preceding graph. The most interesting breakdown of data, however, comes in the analysis of individual stroke competency within each of the proficiency levels. Styles of play become apparent after the analysis of scoring patterns that indicate dominant stroke usage. High subsystem scores in the stroke breakdown is indicative of the stroke patterns used to reach the different achievement levels and a discussion of the data compiled for each achievement level now follows.

Achievement Level I—Professional

The professional level of stroke proficiency is the highest level of stroke adequacy in the game, and is commonly witnessed among world-class players on television as they play at Wimbledon, Forest Hills, or the World Championship of Tennis tour. The average composite score on this level of play is 126.0. In order to reach such a score, a player must not only have developed a highly aggressive style of play, but must also have developed a very efficient style that elicits a minumum number of errors. The graph of the professional shows no negative deficiency in any of the stroke subsystems. The lowest score is a 4.0 in the overhead smash, which is low not because of the player's inability to execute the shot consistently, but because

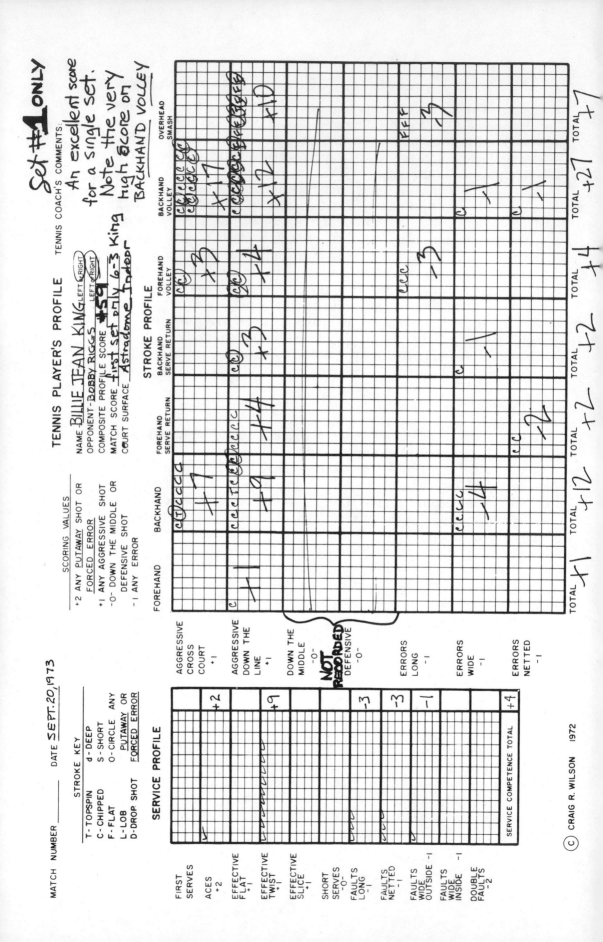

of the fact that the pro is rarely forced to use it. On this level, the lob is used predominantly as a last resort, since the overhead smash is missed so rarely by players of this caliber. It is always a wise strategy to not give any opponent a shot that he is able to execute decisively, a high percentage of the time. The service return scores are 13.1 for the forehand and 10.4 on the backhand, and are the next lowest average on the graph. Again, the scores are not low because of player deficiency. Rather, in the receiving games, the player is on the defensive end of the opponent's most aggressive shot—the serve. On this level, it is very difficult to reverse the initiative of the service, and most professional sets are decided by one service break. The serve is often returned, but is less often returned in a manner capable of reversing the initiative of the play and thereby warranting a rating of "aggressive." Against the professional server, the scores of 13.1 and 10.4 are very respectable. The scores of the professional rise significantly after this point, with the ground strokes and volley all averaging between 15 and 20—forehand 20.5, backhand 16.2, fore-

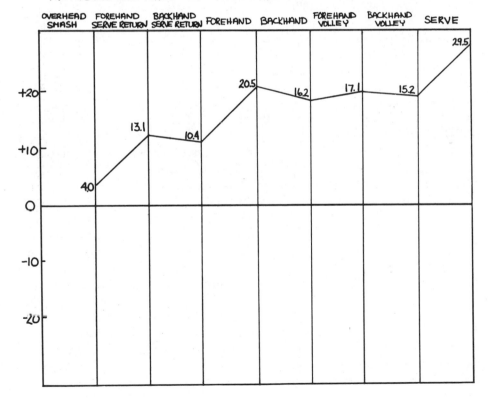

Achievement level: I PROFESSIONAL   COMPOSITE AVERAGE 126.0

hand volley 17.1, backhand volley 15.2. These scores form a close range because of the fact that the player serves and volleys on his service games while occupying a defensive position to the same tactic of the opponent on the receiving games, consequently calling for extensive use of the ground strokes. On both, the forehand remains the dominant side but the difference in the scores is not a large one, with both sides being highly adequate. The difference that does exist is slight and more than likely stems from the early backhand favoritism developed by most beginners. This forehand dominance seems to be widespread, but with notable exceptions such as the great Australian Ken Rosewall and American Grand Slam winner Don Budge preferring use of the backhand. The service is the most aggressive shot of the professional, the average of which is 29.5. It is essential to serve well on this level, since it is the serve that sets the stage for successful play at the net. It is most noteworthy that the scores rise consistently in the progression from left to right on this graph. This highly aggressive but very consistent style of play is ideal. It is interesting that, as one progresses down the ladder of proficiency, the styles of play become noticeably erratic, the documentation of which is readily seen on the following graphs.

Achievement Level II—Championship Tournament
    The player characterizing achievement level II is only a notch under the professional, but there is a noticeable difference between his profile and that of the pro. The overhead smash is .2 of a point higher but no real significance can be made of change that small. It remains a strong shot and is avoided as much as possible by the opposition. The service return scores drop noticeably from 13.1 and 10.4 to 4.0 and 7.0, less than half of that of the pro. The service is still the dominant stroke at this level, but the player's ability to receive the effective serve is considerably less. The pro has developed this portion of his game to a significantly higher degree and can, therefore, put much more pressure on his opponent during the receiving games. This is one of the primary reasons that the professional will consistently defeat the level II championship player. The ground strokes show a similar drop from the pro's 20.5 and 16.2 to 10.8 and 9.6. There is very little difference between them and the scores recorded for the volley, a fact that suggests that this player has a well-diversified game to work from, but that it is one neither as aggressive nor consistent as the pro. The forehand volley dropped 7.1 points to 10.0, and the backhand volley dropped similarly from 15.2 to 13.0. The aggressive games played on the professional level are directly dependent on the player's ability to volley decisively, and the graph depicts this very well. At 21.3, the serve is 8.2 points lower but, nevertheless, remains the highest subsystem score at this com-

Achievement level: II CHAMPIONSHIP TOURNAMENT COMPOSITE AVERAGE 79.9

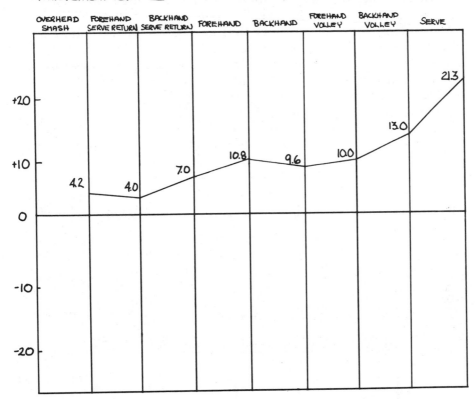

petency level. The player of this ability has no outstanding deficiency, but lacks the elusive ingredient that combines aggressive shot making with control and consistency.

Achievement Level III—Tournament

The average composite score for the achievement level III is 60.5. The overhead-smash average dropped slightly, but insignificantly, to 3.1. The return of serve remains low with the forehand dipping .5 to 3.5, and backhand taking a significant decline from 7.0 to 2.7. The backhand shows itself as a weakness to be exploited among players of this class, and this is particularly apparent in the service return subsystem. The all-court adequacy witnessed on level II has weakened, with the subsystem curve becoming noticeably more erratic. The forehand drive rose from 10.8 to 10.2. The backhand drive is higher as well, likewise rising from 9.6 to 10.2. This fluctuation in the curve is not as contradictory as one might first think, however, since the validity of the curve is restored as soon as one views the consistent decline in the serve and volley scores on the same profile. The level III player centers his attack from the baseline rather than the net, thus necessitating that a much higher percentage of shots be hit from this position. The shots he hits that are aggressive in nature most often come from his ground strokes, and this is reflected in the data and on the graph. The curve does not rise as one progresses through the volley toward the serve. The forehand volley dropped from 10.0 to 6.5, and the backhand from 13.0 to 5.1. These changes are most significant and mark a definite shift in playing styles. It is now possible to observe a reluctance to attack the net as well as a noticeable reliance on the ground strokes. The service average dropped from 21.3 to 13.2. A serve of this type is most often inconsistent, while lacking the variety and/or control to properly set the stage for aggressive professional play at the net. The dominant stroke for this player is the forehand and, at 16.2, is a full three points higher than the serve.

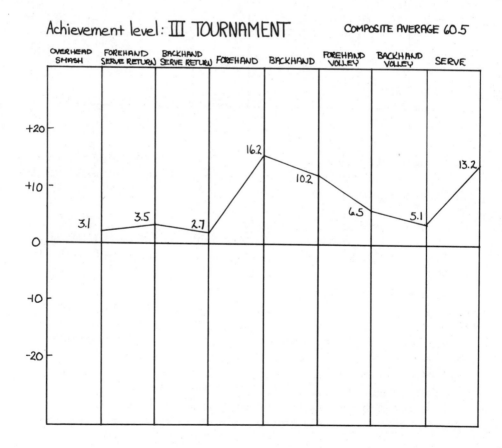

Achievement level: III TOURNAMENT   COMPOSITE AVERAGE 60.5

Achievement Level IV—Advanced

The composite *Profile* average for the advanced player is 38.0. The overhead smash dropped to zero, while both the forehand and backhand service returns dipped into the negative numbers with scores of −.5 and −1.0 respectively. This player does not play the receiving games well, a fact that would seem to indicate that stroke adequacy on this level falls considerably when forced. The service average dropped 3.2 points to 10.0, a score that leaves the serve the second highest score, and one capable of forcing the opponent with an inconsistent service return. The forehand drive is by far the most outstanding shot on this level at 15.7. The backhand is just over half as potent at 8.3, a score that reflects a shot less aggressive and more inconsistent than the forehand. This player's game is firmly implanted on the baseline, where he can force his opposition with his forehand, while reinforcing his left side with an adequate, but only mediocre, backhand. Despite the fact that a shot of this caliber could be

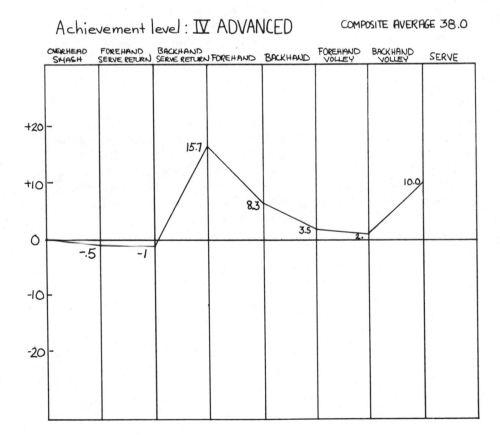

Achievement level: IV ADVANCED   COMPOSITE AVERAGE 38.0

channeled to set the stage for aggressive play at the net, the *Profile* scores of the volley fail to indicate such an inclination. Volley scores dropped over fifty percent, with the forehand dipping from 6.5 to 3.5, and the backhand declining from 5.1 to 2.0. At 10.0, the service score is adequate but not outstanding with extreme force or variety. The service should always be a man's highest subsystem score, and it is at this level that it begins to become subordinate to other parts of the game, in this case the forehand.

Achievement Level V—Intermediate

The average composite score for the level V intermediate player is 18.7. The overhead smash subsystem dropped into the negative number system at −2.3 and indicates a definite lack of support for any inclination a player might otherwise have to play the net. The forehand service return is up from −.5 to +5.6. This is most interesting since it had appeared as though all subsystem scores had entered a predictable dropping trend. This apparent contradiction resolves itself as one notes the fifteen-point drop in service competency from +10.0 to −5.6. The data had showed a consistent drop in service return scores up until this time, since the general stroking ability had lessened at each level, while the serve remained forcing, in the positive number set. This is no longer the case, however, since the intermediate service adequacy suffered such a drastic decline. Because this man faces an uncontrolled service, where the aim is primarily to get the ball in play without faulting, it is often possible to run around many shots, making them on the only real asset at his disposal—the forehand. The sharp decline in service competency has caused this unexpected increase in the forehand service return and does not indicate a contradictory increase in forehand proficiency. The backhand serve return shows little fluctuation, gaining an insignificant .3 of a point from −1.0 to −.7. The forehand drive parallels the forehand return of serve by increasing from 15.7 to 18.1, while the backhand drive dropped considerably from 8.3 to 3.1. The player of intermediate ability plays the game with less purpose and control than any of the other studies examined thus far. These players often find it to their immediate advantage to, at times, run around their backhand side, a fact that is well documented by the increase in the forehand subsystem data. Play at the net must be considered a liability for the intermediate player, since scores for the forehand volley dropped from 3.5 to .8, and the backhand from 2.0 to −.3. The service is no longer capable of lending support to the aggressive tactic of net play, after taking the tremendous drop from +10.0 to −5.6. In light of this service score, it is all but a disadvantage to serve; a considerable liability in view of the fact that a player must serve half of the games played. A service of this type is often incon-

Achievement level: V INTERMEDIATE   COMPOSITE AVERAGE 18.7

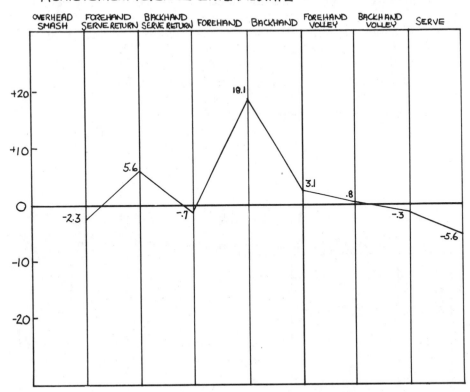

sistent and delivered without purpose or conscious intent other than getting it into the court. It is most interesting, as this analysis of the data nears completion, to review and note the profound influence of the service and how it directly affects the other aspects of a player's stroke development.

Achievement Level VI—Beginner

The composite average of the beginning player is −13.9. Such a score reflects extremely erratic play where keeping the ball in play is the primary concern. The overhead smash rose from −2.3 to −.3, an occurrence that reflects the fact the intermediate player plays the net at times, but in a failing effort, whereas the beginner neither has the ability to play the net or to draw a player of similar ability to the same. He is in a position at the net less than the intermediate, therefore missing and detracting from his score less, as well. The forehand return of serve is up from 5.6 to 7.0, a score that indicates extreme forehand dominance and the backhand service return scores reflect this, dropping from .7 to −3.6. The forehand drive is down

from 18.1 to 13.6 and indicates that while the beginning player re-
lies almost exclusively on his forehand, it is nevertheless a very mediocre shot and one that produces more errors than the intermediate.
The backhand suffered a decline into the negative number system as
it dropped from 3.1 to −1.6. The backhand is a difficult shot for the
beginner to learn and it is directly reflected in the score. The volley
scores remain low, changing very little, with the forehand dropping
from +.8 to −.3 and the backhand from −.3 to –0–. This change is an
insignificant one and reflects well the fact that the intermediate and
beginning players rarely venture to the net, with the times they do
most often ending in a failing experience.

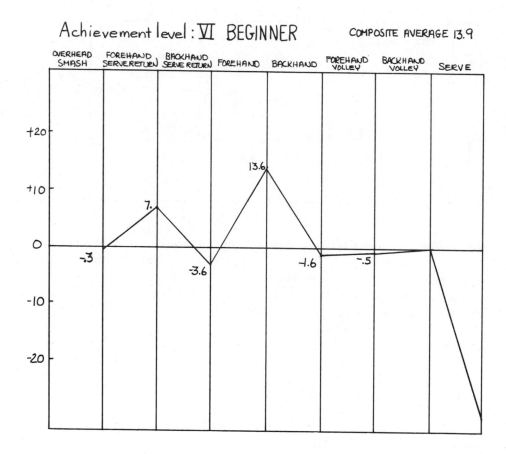

Achievement level : VI BEGINNER   COMPOSITE AVERAGE 13.9

11

THE PLAYER INTERACTION ANALYSIS

The *Tennis Player's Profile* is a record of one player's responses to an opponent's initiatives. It fulfills its designed purpose by giving a descriptive picture of one player as he competes. It does not offer a direct cause-and-effect relationship, nor does it give a point-by-point breakdown of the play. It is possible for two people to chart the same match, each doing a different player, but the result is not a totally objective one, since the value judgments made by two people could never be the same. The system requires a personal value judgment every time a decision is made as to whether a shot should be deemed neutral or aggressive, down-the-line or down-the-middle, etc. It was with this in mind that the *Player Interaction Analysis* was developed. It is a device that allows for the reflection of both sides of a high-intensity encounter, where the concern is purely competitive and centered on the event at hand. In this case, the concept of long-term personal development that underlaid the *Profile* is less of a concern than winning. The education of the tennis player is two-fold, since it is important also to learn the tactics of winning and the whys of losing. The *Player Interaction Analysis* is a practical guide for both.

The *Player Interaction Analysis* was designed from the same basic format as the *Tennis Player's Profile*. Aggressive play is rewarded (+1), neutral play neither rewarded nor punished (−0−), and negative erroring performance punished (−1). Errors negate aggressive shots in the end, thus allowing for a total score for each player, stroke by stroke as well as in total, after the addition and cancellation at the conclusion of the match. The stroke and placement alternatives are located in the same positions as in the original *Profile*. The difference in the systems lies in the way the charts are marked. The *Tennis Player's Profile* is marked with descriptive abbreviations for each shot, while the *Player Interaction Analysis* is marked by numerical subscriptions 1, 2, 3, 4, 5, etc. The first shot of the match, a serve, is marked 1, the return of serve 2, and so on. If, for example, there were five shots hit in the first point, the beginning serve of the second point would be marked 6, the return of serve 7, and so

PLAYER INTER-ACTION ANALYSIS

SET NUMBER _____ DATE _____

POINT BREAKDOWN NOTED BY ANY NUMBER
ENTERED IN ERROR COLUMNS OR BY A
CIRCLE DENOTING A PUTAWAY.

GAME SCORE

1	1
2	2
3	3
4	4
5	5
6	6
7	7

SCORING VALUES
+2 ANY PUTAWAY SHOT
+1 ANY AGGRESSIVE SHOT
-0- DOWN THE MIDDLE OR DEFENSIVE SHOT
-1 ANY ERROR

	LEFT RIGHT		LEFT RIGHT
PLAYER A		PLAYER B	
MATCH SCORE ____		MATCH SCORE ____	
ANALYSIS SCORE ____		ANALYSIS SCORE ____	
COURT SURFACE ____		COURT SURFACE ____	
EVENT ____		EVENT ____	

COMMENTS:

STROKE PROFILE

Column headers: FOREHAND · BACKHAND · FOREHAND SERVE RETURN · BACKHAND SERVE RETURN · FOREHAND VOLLEY · BACKHAND VOLLEY · OVERHEAD SMASH (each with A / B / TOTAL subcolumns)

Rows:
- AGGRESSIVE CROSS COURT +1
- AGGRESSIVE DOWN THE LINE +1
- DOWN THE MIDDLE -0-
- DEFENSIVE -0-
- ERRORS LONG -1
- ERRORS WIDE -1
- ERRORS NETTED -1

SERVICE PROFILE

PLAYER A   PLAYER B

Rows:
- FIRST SERVES
- ACES +2
- EFFECTIVE FLAT +1
- EFFECTIVE TWIST +1
- EFFECTIVE SLICE +1
- SHORT SERVES -0-
- FAULTS LONG -1
- FAULTS NETTED -1
- FAULTS WIDE OUTSIDE -1
- FAULTS WIDE INSIDE -1
- DOUBLE FAULTS -2
- SERVICE COMPETENCE TOTALS

PLAYER INTER-ACTION ANALYSIS
– CAUSE AND EFFECT TRANSLATION –

NAME _____ A or B _____ DATE _____ OPPONENT _____ EVENT _____

Column headers: SERVICE FLAT | SERVICE TWIST | SERVICE SLICE | FOREHAND SERVE RETURN | BACKHAND SERVE RETURN | FOREHAND VOLLEY | BACKHAND VOLLEY | FOREHAND | BACKHAND | OVERHEAD

SHOT SEQUENCES (read down) — TOTALS

SHOT SEQUENCES — TOTALS

SHOT SEQUENCES — TOTALS

PUTAWAYS

PLAYER   A or B
    Shot preceding putaway
SEQUENCE   B or A
    Original initiative of putaway sequence
    A or B

AGGRESSIVE SHOTS

PLAYER   A or B
    Preceding shot
SEQUENCE   B or A
    Original initiative of aggressive sequence
    A or B

ERRORS

PLAYER   A or B
    Immediate cause of error
SEQUENCE   B or A
    Secondary cause of error – shot indirectly responsible for loss of point
    A or B

forth throughout the match. It is best to chart the match using multicolored pens, changing colors once the number sequence reaches 100. Three-digit numbers are difficult to manage and are not easily fitted to the small squares of the chart. While the cause-and-effect relation is in front of the user at the conclusion of the match, it is often more than the average player is willing to do, to sit down and search it out. The *Player Interaction Analysis Sheet* was developed to simplify this chore, and to make interpretation of the data easier. This translation sheet is unique and sets forth a comprehensive theory of the game in itself. It reinforces the *Profile* theory that championship play in tennis occurs in systematic patterns, and further theorizes that the critical shot in these sequences often occurs before its conclusion, by opening the court or allowing it to be opened, by a shot previous to the ultimate putaway and end of the point. Every shot is recorded and abbreviated numerically for concise entrance on the sheet. The translation legend is as follows:

Service Flat	1F
Service Twist	1T
Service Slice	1S
Forehand Service Return	2
Backhand Service Return	3
Forehand Volley	4
Backhand Volley	5
Forehand Drive	6
Backhand Drive	7
Overhead Smash	8

There are three basic sections to this device and they include putaway sequences, aggressive sequences, and erring sequences. All are recorded in terms of the two shots preceding the ultimate conclusion, giving forth a study of considerably more depth. This analysis allows for a cause-and-effect breakdown for every player behavior recorded on the *Player Interaction Analysis*. The data is translated a final time when it is entered into the total columns. At this time it is possible to criticize in mass, any or all, of the positive and negative aspects of the match in question.

The *Player Interaction Analysis* is a tool that allows the player, coach, or pro to identify an additional and entirely different pattern of play. While the *Tennis Player's Profile* identifies dominant stroke patterns, the *Player Interaction Analysis* lends itself to the analysis of the tactical patterns of competitive play. The *Tennis Player's Profile* identifies and categorizes WHAT you see, and the *Player Interaction Analysis* tells you WHY you see it. These tools illuminate two important dimensions of the game of tennis: the first represented by the longitudinal progress study of a player through his career (the *Profile*), and the second offering an in-depth analysis of a specific moment (match) in a player's history (*Interaction Analysis*). The *Tennis Player's Profile* is a teaching aid, a diagnostic or scouting instrument, a statistically significant prediction device, and is a career record that shows longitudinal progress through time. The *Player Interaction Analysis* complements this by serving as an in-depth study of a specific moment in a player's history, giving a cause-and-effect, point-by-point breakdown of the play, as well as serving as an excellent study in tactics.

These methods of objectifying player performance are the first conceptual models of tennis behavior and interaction. This is a new field of inquiry to the game, and I foresee a clear computer capability for analysis of regional styles, tournament difficulty, seeding of players, as well as further breakdown of the competence levels necessary to compete successfully on the different age levels in competition citywide, statewide, sectionally, nationally, and internationally.